Ariel Magidson

# Your Space, Made Simple

Recipes for Approachable, Affordable, and Sustainable Interior Design

# Contents

# Introduction

Maybe you've just moved into a new home and are determined to make it feel uniquely "you." Or maybe you've been living in the same space for years, but it's never quite looked the way you wanted. Whatever has brought you to this book, welcome! I'm glad you're here.

You may have spent hours flipping through fancy interior design books, scrolling past pretty pictures on Pinterest, and wandering down the aisles of home goods stores. Perhaps you already have a vision for how you want your home to look, but you aren't quite sure how to achieve it—or how you'll afford it. More often than not, that decision fatigue probably leads to impulsive purchases you later regret—and to one more trendy throw pillow tossed into your donate pile.

I'm on a mission to put an end to all these common headaches. I want to show you not just what good design looks like, but how to finally achieve it. I want to bring interior design to the masses and challenge my industry's elitist attitude that beautiful home design is only for the uber-wealthy. I want you to leave this book feeling like approachable, affordable, and sustainable design is within your reach.

What follows in this book are my best how-tos for every room of your home. Whether you live in a small apartment in the city or a big house in the suburbs, I've got advice to make every space work for you, not against you.

Part 1 of this book introduces you to my Design Process, breaking down my methodology to teach you the foundations of functional and sustainable design. Then Part 2 dives into my "cookbook" for interior design. Part of the reason I formatted *Your Space, Made Simple* as a cookbook is because I love the challenge of breaking down design into a simple process that can be followed like a recipe. If you have the right ingredients and clear instructions, then you should be able to make something quite similar. And after you've had a little bit of practice, you can add your own spices, a tweak of a step here or there, to come up with something that works even better for you and your space.

The first set of design recipes you'll see are the "Base Palette" recipes. A base palette includes design elements that you can find in nearly every space, such as window treatments, area rugs, and color palettes. It's the tool designers use to create subtle cohesion.

All other recipes are organized by room: entryway, bedroom, living room, dining room, kitchen, bathroom, office, and outdoors. As you browse these sections, you can find recipes that work for your particular space and implement them. I invite you to browse these recipes, find the ones that speak to you, and bring them to your loved ones.

Now before we roll up our sleeves and get to work, let's take a moment to learn what approachable, affordable, and sustainable design is all about . . .

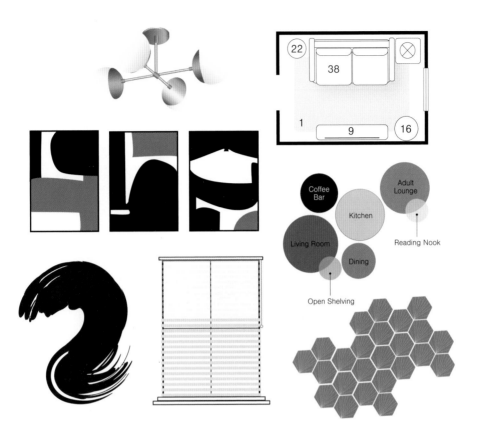

# Approachable

Interior design is often described as a set of rules or "styles" that you're supposed to follow. If there's one key lesson I want you to learn from this book, it's this: style doesn't matter!

Seriously! I mean it! One of the most common questions I get asked is, "What's your style?" and my answer is always, "I don't have one." As a designer, I always see my primary job as creating a space full of *function*. Design is a series of solutions to the specific problems of that space and the people who occupy it. The solutions that work in one context don't always translate to what will work in another context.

On my mission to make design approachable for everyone, I've become best known for my design hacks on social media. I love breaking down the "how" of interior design for anyone to use for free. Everyone should have the opportunity to learn solutions to improve their spaces. While interior design is a complex system that requires education and experience to master, hundreds of design elements and principles are simple and easy to adapt for anyone, at any skill level.

# Affordable

Design is about making your space work for your individual needs and helping you to feel the way you want to feel in your own space. Too often I've seen my fellow designers create incredible spaces for clients that they're unable to access for themselves. I strongly believe there's no reason that interior design can't be made to be affordable for everyone. Here are a few ways I like to combat the extravagance of interior design in favor of affordability:

**SOURCE FROM VENDORS AT EVERY PRICE RANGE:** We don't all have the luxury of buying full-out custom or high-end furniture, and that's okay! Don't be afraid to invest in the things you care about and will use constantly, like your sofa or dining table. The things you use less, spend less on—like table lamps, side tables, and throw pillows.

**RELY ON YOUR NETWORK:** If you're new to this whole interior design thing, you probably have a list of hundreds of questions, and an even longer to-do list. Write them all down! Think about who you know that might be able to help you answer a few questions off your list. Designers work collaboratively with each other, and we rely on advice from other designers to bounce ideas off of—why not do the same within your own network of people? Even a close friend with great taste could be a fantastic resource!

**GET LOUD:** Who said you can't reach out to designers you admire? Send them DMs or emails and ask for advice. You might be surprised with the level of support you receive! Even if you only pay for an hour or two, that can be the difference between a messy home and a functional, beautiful one. Raise your voice and see what you can learn.

Design is about making your own rules,
*not* fitting yourself into someone else's.

# Sustainable

The interior design industry is responsible for millions of tons of waste—per year. Every single year, waste from furniture and interior-related materials gets dumped in our landfills.

But interior designers can have a much bigger impact on climate change than most even realize. While still in school, I earned LEED AP ID+C and WELL AP certifications so that I could specialize in environmentally friendly design. Now, at Ariel Arts, we aim to source at least 90 percent of our materials sustainably. I encourage you to do the same!

What do I mean by sustainable? Here are a few ways you can make sure your own designs are sustainable, too:

**REUSE, UPCYCLE, BUY VINTAGE, RECYCLE, AND DONATE:** The first rule of sustainability is to make as little waste as possible. I encourage my clients and audiences to use as many pieces that they already own as possible. Sometimes, a fresh coat of paint or a good steam clean is all you need to give new life to an old piece. For those items you know no longer work for you, donating or recycling them is the best way to prevent them from entering landfills. And when you can, go vintage! There are so many beautiful secondhand items out there that don't require any new materials to be made.

**LOOK FOR ENVIRONMENTALLY FRIENDLY LABELS:** Increasingly, consumers consider a company's environmental footprint before becoming customers. But greenwashing— when a company spends more time and money marketing themselves as environmentally conscious rather than truly investing in sustainable practices—can deceive customers trying to put their money where their values are. When shopping for new items, I look for a few labels that help us determine whether products were made sustainably: FSC Wood (Forest Stewardship Council is considered the "gold standard" of wood harvesting)[1]; GREENGUARD (certification that ensures interior products are low in chemical emissions, decreasing indoor pollution levels)[2]; Sustainable Furnishing Council (a membership organization for companies committed to creating, selling, and promoting sustainable furnishings products); and Cradle to Cradle (certification for products that are safe, circular, and responsibly made)[3].

**REDUCE ADDITIONAL WASTE:** Anything you purchase has the potential to create more waste and environmental consequences. To mitigate this, I recommend looking for products that are locally made by locally owned businesses. For most of my clients, "Made in USA" is a good start. But you can find incredible things even closer to home! By shopping locally, you reduce the waste and emissions associated with shipping products. Smaller businesses also tend to produce less waste in the creation of products, as they rarely overproduce and have a tighter supply chain. This goes for handmade, artisan-made, and small-batch products as well.

x

## PART 1

The Design Process

# CHAPTER ONE

# Function

I know you're excited to dive into colors, textures, furniture, and decor! But to set you up for success, start with function. Why function first?

- It makes everything else straightforward. By determining your needs from your space from the outset, you can effortlessly filter out hundreds of potential choices and pick from just those that you know will work for you.

- You'll be happier in your space. Creating spaces in your home that work for your unique needs can help make you calmer and happier. It will also be easier to live your life the way you want to live it!

- It empowers you to get it right the first time. You do not want to go through the process of designing a beautiful new space just to find out it doesn't really work for you, and then have to do it all over again!

- It's more sustainable. Recall that we dump millions of tons of furniture waste every year. Trends are fleeting. They change quickly. Instead of looking for what's trendy (in other words, what will just go out of style next year), design should be created to last for years to come. You'll be happier longer and create less waste!

Generally, two important aspects determine your functionality needs: 1) How you already live your life, and 2) What makes you, well . . . you!

Lastly, before we dive in, I must note that this process will only work if you're totally honest with yourself. To do that, you have to make a promise first: *this is a judgment-free zone!*

Seriously, stop listening to the noise. Stop listening to advice that doesn't truly resonate with you. Whoever you are and however you live is worthy. It really is! We have all been taught that there is a way we should look, talk, express interest, or just be. The design problem with that engrained approach is that if you try to mold yourself into some unachievable ideal, you'll create a space that's meant for someone else. It might be beautiful, but it won't be you.

So, let's make something that's just for the unique, real, and beautiful you!

Do you promise to get honest? Do you promise not to criticize yourself? Woohoo! Grab something to write with so that you can take notes as you read through these sections. Let's get started!

# How Do You Live Your Life?

Let's take stock of your habits. What are your frequent habits? Your occasional habits? Your aspirational habits? I like to categorize habits as "daily," "workweek," "weekend," and "special occasion."

While plenty of your habits are easy to identify, you might not be as aware of others. Start by jotting down what you can now and then try to observe your day-to-day behavior over the next week or so. As you notice more habits, add them to your notes.

## Daily Habits

Most of our daily, at-home habits happen at the beginning and then end of the day—when we're home! Here are some example daily habits:

**BEGINNING OF THE DAY**: put on slippers; drink coffee or tea; catch up on social media or the news; exercise

**END OF THE DAY**: drop backpacks, coats, keys, and other items by the front door or mudroom; kick off shoes; make dinner; watch TV or read

As you write down these habits, you can start to see how design will come into play. I can't tell you how many people I know who've lost their keys from time to time—I used to, too! So what's the design solution? Dedicate a bowl or hooks by the door for keys, and you'll always know where they are. Create a healthy habit of having a place to put them each time and you won't lose your keys anymore. This is the perfect example of identifying that annoying habit and creating a new healthy one out of it.

You can also plan for aspirational daily habits. Remember to be realistic and gentle here. We're not trying to mold ourselves into some superhuman version! These aspirations should be small changes that will make you feel a little happier or calmer.

One example of this is that when we first moved in together, my fiancé would have a quick cup of coffee in the morning and then leave for work right away. But the rushed coffee before dashing off led to stressful mornings. So, we set a new intention to have coffee together each morning and spend a little extra time together before work, just the two of us. To encourage us, we designed the dining nook in our home to be welcoming and cozy, encouraging us and our guests to sit and visit. This small change has made a huge difference! Now we can't start our day without, "morning time"—it changed our behavior for the better.

See how design and well-being are linked? It's not just about having time. It's about creating time—and creating the space to take that time.

Think about how interior design can help you create the time you're craving.

16

# Habit *Tracker*

**Morning Habits:**

Morning coffee with my partner. = Prioritize a coffee nook.

**Daily Habits:**

Commute to work everyday? = Prioritize a drop-off console.

**Evening Habits:**

Decompress after work? = Prioritize a cozy living room.

# Work From *Home*?

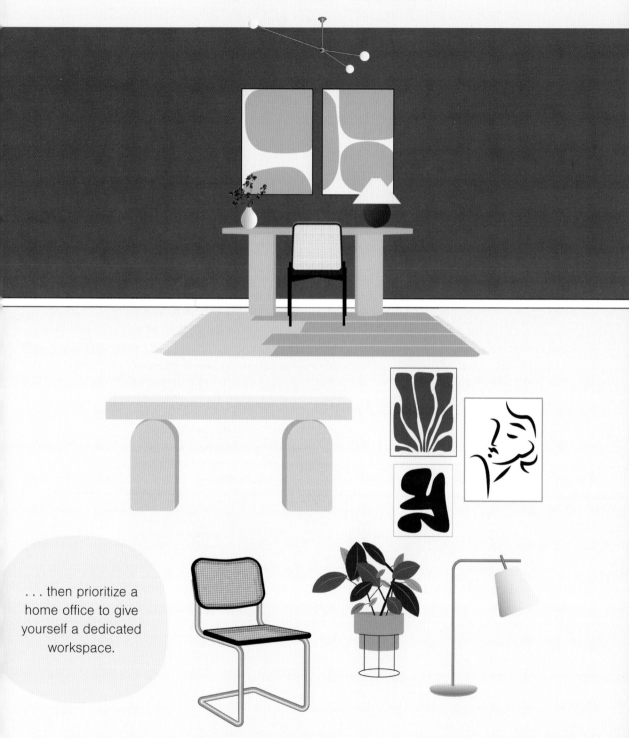

. . . then prioritize a home office to give yourself a dedicated workspace.

# Weekday Habits

Many of our morning and evening habits have to do with work, school, and all the other responsibilities that come during the week. For this section, make notes about what you do during the week and how that affects your habits at home.

## Do You Commute?

Commuters tend to need to take things with them, like a laptop or a lunch. That means collecting things before leaving the house in the morning, then dropping them somewhere when you come home.

If you're a commuter, think about what you need to gather before leaving the house in the mornings. What changes would make your morning routine easier or less stressful? Would it help to have a basket for your work items near the door? Are there rituals, like reading the paper or practicing yoga, that would help you feel prepared for your day?

## Do You Work From Home?

When your home and your office are the same place, it can be easy to feel like you can't escape work. Trust me, I know about living in your workplace—I worked out of our six-hundred-square-foot condo for two years during the pandemic. There's nowhere to escape in that confined a space!

19

The beauty of design, though, is that you don't need to "escape" your work to create separation. If you have the space for a home office with a door, you can close the door at the end of the workday. There are plenty of other ways to create separation. For a few days, observe your weekday habits and take note of how you tend to start your workday: what signals you're "on" for the day? And what helps you feel like you're done for the day?

If you work from home, think about small rituals that will help you mark work time, like lighting a candle when work begins and blowing it out when it's over. Some people prefer to have a shelf or basket where their laptops and other work-related accoutrement can be easily put away to end the workday. Out of sight, out of mind.

Of course, if you work from home, you will also want to think about where you prefer to work. Do you work at a desk, dining table, or sofa? Or do you move around? Think about where you tend to work so that you can create the space you need to be productive there. This will come in handy when you're considering furniture and lighting!

## Do You Have Kids?

If you have kids—or if you're responsible for others in your household during the week—there are many other habits to consider. Jot down notes about what you're responsible for in the mornings and evenings. Are you packing lunches and backpacks? Do the kids need help picking out outfits or getting dressed? Are there things they tend to misplace, like shoes or books?

- Think about the items your kids need to start and end their day successfully and how creating more structure around those routines could make them easier for everyone. Some families find that organizing clothes by outfit instead of clothing type helps kids get ready on their own. Creating dedicated hooks, baskets, or shelves for backpacks, shoes, and jackets also helps prevent misplacing things in the rush to school.

- Also think about how your family tends to spend their weekday mornings and evenings. Some families like to eat together at breakfast and/or dinner. Others like to have separate quiet times. Children might be more likely to play with toys at certain times and watch TV at other times. Take notes about how your family's weekdays look so that you can design around how you already live your lives. Remember to be honest and write down your actual habits!

**WHAT DO YOUR EVENINGS LOOK LIKE?** Don't forget to think about your regular evening habits during the weekdays. Some people are more likely to go home and cook, while others are more likely to order takeout or dine out. Do you tend to prefer quiet evenings at home or to meet up with friends?

**HOW DO YOU DECOMPRESS?** We all need more downtime. It's a symptom of the times we live in. But I have good news for you! Design can help you with that too!

A good exercise to create more time to decompress is to take note of the things that help you relax. If these aren't regular habits for you yet, we can help you prioritize relaxation more often. On days you do feel more relaxed, how are you spending your time? What activities do you engage in? Here are some examples of what I'm talking about:

- Drinking a cup of tea or cocktail

- Watching TV or reading a book

- Doing a hobby like knitting

- Calling a friend or family member

- Working out, taking a walk, or practicing yoga

Whatever you do to decompress, think about what kind of space or items you need access to: a comfy chair, space for exercise, or a ready-to-go gym bag. Think about what would encourage you to engage in more of these decompression activities. Would it be helpful if the comfy chair was in your bedroom, where you often spend time at the end of the day? Would setting up a tea station or a minibar entice you to have that end-of-day drink?

# Weekend Habits

It can be a bit harder to pinpoint your weekend habits because they tend to fluctuate more than weekday habits. Don't try to be too ambitious with this. Variations in life's demands and social calendars can make it more difficult to build new habits for weekends. Instead, be gentle with yourself and note the habits you do have. Here are some examples:

- Engaging in a hobby like gardening or crafting

- Entertaining friends and family for barbeques or meals

- Leisure activities like napping, reading, and watching TV

What makes you feel like it's a weekend? For some people, weekends are all about visiting with others, either by having them over or meeting them out in the world. For many parents, weekends tend to be about kids' sports games and playdates. Whatever your weekends look like, that's great! Remember that this is a judgment-free zone. Be honest. Embrace your habits so that your space helps you live your authentic life.

# Special Occasions

What are your special occasions? I love celebrating with friends and family. I'm Jewish and my fiancé is Muslim, so we have lots of holidays to celebrate—often with good food!

Many families have traditions, rituals, or common activities they engage in for special occasions. When determining your own, think broadly. They don't have to be holidays; they might be your monthly girls' night, an annual visit from a relative, or the Super Bowl. What are your special occasions? Jot them down! Considering how special occasions relate to interior design:

- **SEATING**: Do you like to host large gatherings, intimate gatherings, or both? Do you like to host around a table? Where will you need seating? Don't forget to think about seating height. If you need to repurpose your existing seating for a dining table, stools will be too tall, and ottomans will be too short.

- **BEDS**: If you host guests at your house overnight, consider options for guest beds. Of course, a guest room with a bed is often ideal. But there are other options: hideaway beds, air mattresses, and comfy sofas.

- **FLEXIBILITY**: Unless you host all the time, you can look for pieces that have multiple purposes. For example, an extendable dining table will allow for flexible dinner parties but fold down to a size that accommodates more space.

- **ACCESSIBILITY**: Consider your guests and their varying needs, especially those with disabilities, babies, or who require special seating.

# Love *Hosting?*

. . . then prioritize an outdoor space for friends and family to enjoy.

# What Makes You . . . YOU!

Now that we've established your habits and your needs for your home, let's explore what makes you who you are. Style isn't the only design aspect that makes your space feel like a home. It's about embracing objects that feel familiar and inspiring, spaces that give off the vibes you're seeking, and the flexibility for you to grow in the space how you want to.

## Are You an Introvert, Extrovert, or Ambivert?

I am a huge introvert! Not everyone realizes this, given that my face is all over social media, but it's true. I need lots of quiet time, and when I visit with friends and family, I prefer very small gatherings. If you like personality tests, you can determine your introvert-to-extrovert scale with one of the hundreds available online.

For our purposes, you really don't need a quiz. All you need to do is ask yourself is this: When I'm at home, do I feel most comfortable when it's quiet and I'm alone (or with a few people) or when it's noisy and I'm around a lot of people? Or do I need both quiet and noisy times to enjoy my home?

### Introverts

Where are my introverts? We want quiet! We want small, cozy nooks; places to cuddle up and read; small dining spaces; and space to do things on our own. Think about when you feel most comfortable and recharged. Jot down notes about the type of space, lighting, sound, and furniture that would help you feel recharged in an introvert haven.

### Extroverts

Hey, extroverts, where's the party? Do you love to host and have lots of people over? How can you make your space accommodate the kinds of gatherings you enjoy? Do you also love to go out into the world and be around people ? Jot down some notes about how your space can accommodate how often you like to come and go.

### Ambiverts

Do you think of yourself as both an extrovert and an introvert? Do you need quiet time to recharge as much as you need loud, crowded experiences to energize you? For my ambivert clients—and for households that need to accommodate both introverts and extroverts—I recommend creating separate spaces for different activities. You might need a flexible living room to accommodate lots of guests. But try to make space for a quiet reading nook elsewhere, so that you can truly find that quiet solo time to decompress.

# Career

Our careers often share deep ties with our identities and how we spend our time. When you reflect on your career, consider what you need at home for your job, what career-related items or spaces you want to have (or not have) around, and what you need to decompress.

## What Do You Need for Your Job?

Depending on your profession, you might need to have dedicated space or storage for equipment or paperwork, such as a filing cabinet. If you ever work from home, you likely have electronics and accessories that need a home so that they don't clutter your space. You'll also want to reflect on the kind of environment that's most conducive to your work. Some people prefer a minimal, clean feeling for their desk space, which means you should allocate storage above and around your desk so that you can prevent clutter. Other people like to have lots of little tchotchkes around them; these folks will do better with open shelving above their desk so that they can have the things around them that make them happy and inspired, while also maintaining plenty of surface space for work.

## What Do You Need to Decompress?

Everyone needs to decompress after work. Some people will come home and do the very thing they do all day—ever hear of those chefs who come home and bake? Others . . . ahem, me . . . need to do anything but what they did during the day. When I'm done for the day, I don't want to see any designs, floor plans, or specifications lists anywhere. Catch me hiding in a blanket on the couch—I need a calm, quiet place to escape.

In your notes, jot down how you prefer to decompress and what you need to do that. You might also want to take note of what you'd like to avoid when it's time to decompress.

### Reminder: Be Honest with Yourself!

I know I sound like a broken record here, but it's so important that you be honest with yourself when designing spaces that work best for you. Maybe you wish you meditated every night, but if your actual desires are to catch up on your favorite show or read a book, then write that down. The goal is to make your space work for the real you!

# Culture

We've spared hardly any details exploring our habits, but your life comprises more than your routines. When designing your ideal space, you'll also want to explore your heritage, traditions, neighborhood, family of origin, and family of choice. For this section, as you take notes, think about the things that you love about your culture and the things that bring you comfort, pride, and joy. Here are some things to consider:

**HERITAGE**: What is your racial, ethnic, religious, and geographic background? What makes you proud of these parts of yourself?

**TRADITIONS**: What traditions in your life do you love most? How frequently do you engage in these traditions (daily, weekly, monthly, annually)? What, in your environment, would help support and remind you of your traditions?

**FAMILY AND FRIENDS**: Which people in your life are most important to you? What reminders of them do you want to have around?

**FOOD**: If you like to cook your favorite foods (or someone in your house does!), what must your kitchen accommodate? American kitchens typically have insufficient space for spices, which is problematic for many cuisines. Consider the amount of storage space you'll need to make the foods you love.

Once you write down the many aspects that make up your unique cultural experience, there are many ways to incorporate these into your home. Consider objects, like photographs of people and places, books from or about your culture, and art and textiles that represent your culture. You can also use objects that come from the places or people you noted—things such as locally made or sourced artwork, furniture, decor, and foods.

Where you live can determine aspects of your culture, too. I had a client who moved to a neighborhood where no cars were allowed, only golf carts. There was a drinking culture in the area because no one had to drive, and she wanted me to incorporate that into her design. Other neighborhoods are more conducive to being outdoors, eating certain foods, or hanging out on stoops. Most of what you love about where you live—and what you want to escape from in your neighborhood—can be considered in how you design your home.

29

# More Questions to Think About

So much goes into who you are and how you live your life. Here are a few more things you might take note of when you're thinking about how to design your home to work for you.

**WHAT INSPIRES YOU?** Is there memorabilia, art, or other reminders that inspire you? What do you like to look at?

**HOW DO YOU WANT TO FEEL IN YOUR SPACE?** Many of us want to feel comfortable at home, but we must think beyond that. Do you want to feel calm, energized, productive, happy? Your answer will likely vary by room. Once you've identified how you want to feel, think about the things that help you feel that way. What textures, colors, objects, sounds, or lighting help you to feel this way?

**HOW DO YOU FEEL ABOUT CHANGE?** Some of us crave change! I change up my space all the time, so I initially designed a space that allows for that. I have a sofa with different washable covers, artwork to swap around the house, and a picture frame TV to display different art. However, some people absolutely hate change. If this is you, make sure to take your time with your design so that you can create a space you'll be happy with for many years.

**WHAT ARE YOUR SHORT-TERM AND LONG-TERM PLANS?** If you know you will be moving in the next few years, try to plan for flexible furniture that can be used in a new space or items that you know you'll be able to sell down the road. (Remember, our climate depends on minimizing landfill, so try your best not to throw things away.) If you plan to be in your space for the long term, invest in the space and take your time making it exactly how you want it.

Invest in your space and take your time
making it *exactly* how you want it.

# CHAPTER TWO

# Sustainability & Wellness

The bad news first . . .

There is no doubt that the furniture and interiors industry has had a negative impact on our environment. The EPA reports that, in 2018, more than nine million tons of furnishings were added to our landfills, with that number likely increasing every year.[4] Every. Single. Year.

Our landfills are full of relatively new furniture due to the rise of fast furniture. These products are mass produced and sold quickly and cheaply, but they tend to break or diminish in quality quickly. In fact, one estimation says that most of the furniture in landfills was made less than ten to fifteen years ago. We must do better!

But don't despair!

Here's the good news: interior design can be produced and practiced sustainably. And, when done well, design can contribute to your overall mental and physical wellness.

In modern Western cultures, we have become peoples of materialism and overconsumption. Some might think interior designers must appreciate materialism, since it seems to go hand-in-hand with outfitting new spaces, but that doesn't have to be the case. I sometimes suggest my clients get new items, sure. But my designs are about minimizing waste, sourcing sustainable materials, finding ways to offset our current environmental impact, and designing to minimize future environmental impact.

Is anything here new?

Actually . . . not really. Not what you expected me to say? Sustainable design is as old as humanity, taking us back to our roots in nature. Indigenous cultures around the world still practice many of the suggestions you'll read in this section.

Sustainable design isn't new thinking; it's rediscovering how we used to live. So, let's get back to our roots.

# Biophilia

Do you ever notice that you're calmer or happier in certain natural settings, like at the beach or in a park? Have you ever noticed that colors, smells, and objects that come from or remind you of those settings also make you feel calmer or happier?

Coined by psychoanalyst Erich Fromm and further developed by Edward O. Wilson,[5] biophilia is the theory that humans crave nature because we come from nature. Therefore, when we bring nature into our spaces, we become happier. You can bring nature into your home with plants or natural elements, like wood and stone. But you can do so in less obvious ways, too. The same biophilic impact comes from symbolic elements, like artwork and earth tones.

▶ **PRO TIP:** Biophilic design won't go out of style! If you look at interior design over many decades, you'll see that the closer elements are to nature, the less likely they are to go out of style. Plants never go out of style. Organic earth tones don't go away. While different finishing stains go in and out of style, wood itself is always in style. Incorporating nature into your design will help to create a happier environment and last much longer, while trends come and go. Generally, the longer our things last, the less we contribute to landfills and harmful production.

34

# Long-Term Thinking

We're guaranteed one thing in life: change. Everything changes, whether we want it to or not. Designing sustainably means being open to change.

Hang on! Isn't sustainability about keeping things as long as possible and trying not to buy too many new things?

That's part of it. One of the most important components of sustainability is using long-term thinking and adopting a growth mindset. The longer you can keep something, the less you contribute to production, shipping, and landfills. First, you will be more likely to utilize materials for the long term if you truly love them and they best serve your needs. Second, acknowledging, from the outset, that your needs will change over time will help you select items that will adapt with you.

## An Even Bigger Picture

To be truly sustainable, you'll have to take an even longer-term view of the materials you select in your design. Think about where the products came from, how they will be used, and what will happen to them once you're done with them. This concept is called Cradle to Cradle and is a certification you can look for in the products you purchase. (More on what labels to look for in this chapter.)

When we bring nature into our spaces, we become *happier*.

# Conscious Consumption

Products that are mass-produced and/or shipped overseas are worse for the environment. It's an unfortunate truth. But there are so many alternatives. Support the environment and your community by shopping for products that are locally and artisanally made. Consider thrifting or antiquing. Hand-me-downs are always a great option, too. Furniture from grand-parents makes for great conversation pieces!

# Reuse & Repurpose

Save money and limit your environmental impact! What goodies do you already have in your current space? Most likely, you have furniture and decor that can be incorporated into your new design. If there are pieces you're happy with as-is, then use those when creating your overall design. If you have items that are in good condition, but you're not happy with them as-is, consider how to repurpose them or add a little DIY elbow grease to upgrade them. Ask yourself the following questions:

- Instead of a new sofa, could I get a sofa cover?

- Could I paint that cabinet and add some new hardware instead of buying a new credenza?

- If I painted, reupholstered, or added new pillows or decor, would this piece work for me?

**REPURPOSING BONUS:** you'll love your things longer if you had a hand in creating them!

# Efficiencies

So-called "efficient" technologies aren't truly sustainable, but they are a step in the right direction. We use a lot of energy for our various technologies: TVs, computers, phones, and other devices. It's vital to adopt a mindset that looks at efficiency as truly considering how we can take less from the environment and give more.

| Items that *reduce* consumption: | Items that give *more*: |
|---|---|
| • Water-efficient toilets and faucets | • Plants that clean the air |
| • Energy-efficient appliances | • Solar panels to create additional energy |
| • Natural light (meaning less interior lighting needed during the day) | • Donations to your local community |

# Carbon Offsetting

Everyone should do their best to minimize their environmental impact, but the reality is that to live, we must consume, and consumption of almost any kind has a negative impact on the environment. When redesigning your space, consider looking into carbon offsetting. It's not the perfect solution—nothing really ever is—but it's certainly a step in the right direction. Many companies can help you calculate your carbon footprint and suggest a donation amount that will go towards carbon reduction. Although, offsetting doesn't fix the entire world's problems. If you're overconsuming or purchasing from companies that release massive amounts of emissions and try to balance that with carbon offsets, that isn't truly the point of this entire thing, is it? It's all about balance.

# How to Find Sustainable Products

Here's a list of the certifications and labels I look for when sourcing products for my clients.

**NOTE**: This is my list as of the time I'm writing this book. Certifications and descriptions change all the time, so check online for more information!

## Sustainable *Shopping* Keywords:

- Small Batch
- Artisan Made
- Reclaimed
- Vintage
- Upcycled

- Cradle to Cradle
- Made in the US
- BIPOC/Minority-Owned Businesses
- Sustainable Furnishings Council
- Locally Owned and Local Shipping

### A Note About Injustice

Environmental injustice is social injustice. Negative impacts on our planet are more likely to affect lower-income and minority communities. To make matters worse, many good sustainability practices are expensive and out of reach for those most impacted. Those of us with the privilege to be able to make more sustainable choices must do so to make a difference for all of us. Use the privilege you have to lessen your impact on the environment and spend your money wisely to improve the lives of others. Let's do better together.

# Be WELL

Be good to yourself! Make your space one of a kind, all your own, so that it serves your physical, emotional, and spiritual well-being. Be well in your space.

Before finishing design school, I was one of the youngest people to become a LEED AP, a certification built upon the idea of building and creating in a more sustainable manner. I later studied to become a WELL AP. This certification is based on a set of design standards that support individuals' overall well-being with the underlying tone of sustainable practices. And you can use these too!

## Just Breathe

The more choice you have within a space, the more in control you'll feel. So, what does that mean? The ability to change the room's temperature with minimal effort, or allowing fresh air in at any given moment, creates a calm and relaxed environment. Operable windows, fans, and HVAC vents give you flexibility with temperature and ventilation. Fresh, clean air is best for all of us. You can bring some of that inside with plants that give off oxygen and air purifiers to help with allergies and pollution. Think about humidifiers when and where the climate is dry and dehumidifiers in other spaces subject to mold and mildew. It's all about controlling your breath to the way you like it.

41

## Drink More

Water is life! You can leverage your design to help you drink plenty of water every day. How do you like your water—cold or room temp? Purified or tap? In a bottle or cup? Incorporate your preferences into your design. For example, if you're like me and drink more water when it's in a bottle, then keep a designated water bottle close to your sink with a purifier spout. Or, if you're more likely to drink water if it's cold, get a refrigerator with a built-in water dispenser or use a water-filtering pitcher you can keep in the fridge.

## Nourish

In the age of fast, overprocessed foods, our culture doesn't encourage healthy eating as much as convenience. But proper nourishment helps us live happier, healthier lives. Even if you buy junk food or prefer to eat out often, you can use your design to help you make better choices.

Keep healthier foods at your eye level (even if your refrigerator isn't designed that way). Prewash fruits and vegetables so that you can just grab and eat them when you see them. Keep the less healthy snacks further away and out of sight—up high in a pantry or down low in drawers. Try to make it easier on yourself and your household to be nourished.

# Light It Up

Healthy and well-balanced light has a huge impact on your well-being. But we must consider a few factors to create a balanced space: natural lighting, artificial lighting, control, and color temperature.

## Natural Lighting

Natural lighting is vital for our overall health. Think about how you can create an environment that puts you closer to natural light. How can you accentuate your windows to make them feel larger than life? For spaces with limited natural light, such as a room with a very small window, add many touch points of lighting so you can control how much or how little light gets into the space. Lean into the space with limited light and create a mood out of it. Spaces with lots of natural light tend to become very dark at night, so consider how artificial lighting can play into this when the sun isn't out.

## Artificial Lighting & the Power of Three

There are three types of lighting: ambient, task, and accent. Having various touch points of each type in your space will make it feel more complete. This is how you can create a strong mood in various spaces. Consider how calm spaces vary from those you feel more awake in. You can learn about where and how to use each type in the base palette section on page 74. Remember that the more choice you have within a space, the more you will feel in control of your environment. Morning and evening are very different from one another, so consider dimmability or having various touch points of light to set a specific mood during different times of day.

## Color Temperature

Wait, light has a temperature? Yes, yes it does. Ever been in a space that feels like a bright white hospital or a yellow cave? Something's not right there; the color of each light isn't balanced. The color of lighting has a huge impact on sleep, productivity, mood, and even eating patterns. It's not about the fixture type; it's all about the bulb! Here's how to ensure you have even color temperatures in each space:

- LIVING & DINING ROOMS: 2700-3000K (a space for relaxing & conversing)

- BEDROOMS: 2700-3700K (limiting the blue light for a good night's sleep)

- BATHROOMS: 3000-4000K (keep things as natural as possible while getting ready)

- KITCHEN & OFFICES: 4000-4500K (bright light for chopping & to keep you focused)

- OPEN CONCEPT SPACES (KITCHEN, LIVING, DINING): 3000-4000K (you need balance between the calm and focused lighting—consider dimmability for these spaces for more control)

# *Artificial* Lighting Options

Ambient Lighting:

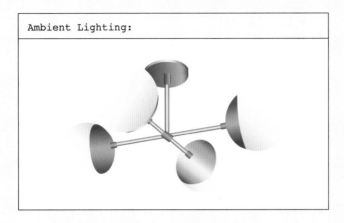

Task Lighting:

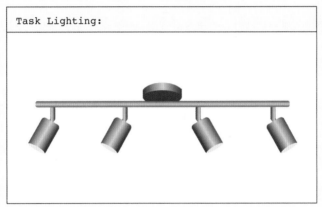

Accent Lighting:

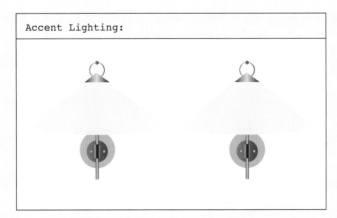

# Move It

We all know that movement is an important part of physical well-being. But did you also know that the freedom to easily move around is tied to your mental well-being? In design, this means encouraging positive movement—like getting up and walking around in the middle of the workday—and ensuring there's plenty of space to get around so that you don't have to climb over things or squeeze through tight spaces. Look back at the Function section (page 14) for more on designing a space that encourages you to move. Also, check out the Accessible Living recipe (page 64) to help you design your space with the right amount of room to move freely.

# I Heard That

How much noise do you like to have around you? Are there certain sounds you enjoy? Of course there are! Sound helps to set a mood, and certain ones can help you focus or stay calm. Some sounds might be irritating, like outside noises or loud appliances. Other sounds might be pleasant, like a quiet fountain or your favorite music. To make spaces quieter, use area rugs, soft furnishings, and sound panels to dampen noise. Sound panels are especially helpful in a den where people might be watching loud movies. If you like to have consistent sounds, consider installing speakers to play the music you love or white noise machines to bring ambient, calming noises to your space.

If you're not sure what kind of sound you want in your space, think about other spaces you visit and what sounds you hear there. For example, spas often play tranquil music and have trickling water sounds. In drug and grocery stores, you're more likely to hear soft pop music. Sound plays an important role in most environments. Recall the ones that make you feel how you want to feel in your space and think about how to incorporate that into your design.

# Living in a Material World

Earlier in the chapter, I talked about prioritizing furniture and decor made sustainably for the earth. Those materials aren't just better for the earth; they're better for you, too! What you bring into your home affects the air you breathe and your overall well-being. Look out for VOCs (volatile organic compounds), which are materials that release toxins into the air. These can release harmful chemicals for years. Some likely sources can be carpet glue, composite woods/MDF, flame-retardant chemicals, memory foam, paint, and some air fresheners. Try to look for products that are formaldehyde-free, VOC-free, or low-VOC emission.

# Your Unique Needs

While this book can't cover every possible need you might have for your design, keep in mind that you can incorporate your (and your family's) unique needs into your own design.

For example, studies have shown that interior design can support people with ADHD, depression, those with physical challenges, and those with special day-to-day needs.[6] The importance of communication within a space and the perception of the space overall is what has massive impacts on overall health. It's about creating a space that works with you, not against you.

Open-plan homes with easy sight lines can support individuals who are deaf or hard of hearing, encouraging more communication at home. Spaces with ample area to move around in if you are blind or in a wheelchair allow these individuals to easily flow through a room without bumping into things. Learn more about accessible living here on page 64.

Many people with ADHD have object permanence—the belief that if I don't see it, it's not there. Consider the organization of your home and the perception of cleanliness to make things feel more in control. This doesn't always need to be baskets and bins; it can be closed cabinets or open shelves with visual cues of what goes where. This can mean having lots of items, each with a specific place to go, or very few items that are all within sight.

It's known that clutter can contribute to our overall mental health by releasing cortisol and triggering the fight or flight mode. How can you keep the things around you that you love without it feeling like clutter? Sometimes this can mean narrowing down the items you have; or just organizing the location of where you put things away.

Don't think of your needs as obstacles to get rid of, but rather as elements of design. Consider the individuals in your household and their physical, emotional, and mental needs. With a little thought—and maybe a little research—you can design to support those needs. Your space will be uniquely you and designed with long-term sustainability when you plan for them.

There isn't a one-solution-fits-all here. The truth is that it's about being honest with yourself and your loved ones about what brings you peace at home for your unique needs.

# CHAPTER THREE

# Concept vs. Style

Are you more mid-century modern or industrial? Modern farmhouse or Scandinavian? Guess what? I don't care! And that's the last time you'll read "style" names in this book.

## What's a Concept?

Concepts are based on your lifestyle needs and desires, rather than broad-brush categories made up by magazines and marketers. Everyone has a slightly different concept for their own spaces, and that's how it should be.

Every home should not look the same. That's boring AF!

Instead, design your space in such a way that when people enter your home, they get a sense for who you are. Not which magazine or Pinterest posts you like best, but who you are.

## Combine & Integrate

Take stock of your own background and cultural makeup. How many factors contribute to the beautiful, complex human you are? There are so many parts of what make you, you. No one is just one thing.

In the Function section, we touched on your heritage, interests, and habits. These are all parts of your identity. So are your tastes, what you gravitate to and feel inspired by.

It's totally fine if you tend to like one of the standard styles. But, often, you'll discover more if you look a little deeper to see what it is about that style that speaks to you and how to incorporate it with other things that also speak to you. This is how you create a curated, classic look.

Plus, there's no need to use the same design concept for every room. You might want to have a natural, laid-back vibe in your main living area and a dark, moody concept in your bedroom. When thinking about your concept for each space, think about how you want to feel in that space, in addition to how you want to use that space.

Give yourself permission to go bold! My favorite aspect in any house is achieving an element of surprise—to open the door to a powder room and just . . . bam! The unexpected hits you.

49

# Be Mindful of Cultural Appropriation

While developing your concept, it's important to be mindful of cultural appropriation and how it manifests in the interior design industry. Without doing your research, it's easy to accidentally purchase items that exploit the cultures we mean to celebrate. When purchasing items that are traditionally created by a particular culture, such as Indonesian ikat fabrics or Moroccan rugs, prioritize sourcing products that were made by and empower people from those communities, rather than mass-produced replications, which actually exploit those communities.

# You Are Not an Algorithm!

Human beings are complex, emotional creatures. But the places we look for inspiration for our spaces . . . well, those are based on algorithms—at least, if they're through the internet. Computers can help you explore concepts, but they will not help you discover your unique concept that makes your space one of a kind.

Incoming design secret! (Shhh!) Designers know that the internet is a great source for design inspiration, but we can't use just one source. To create a concept like a designer, seek out inspiration from many sources, like magazines, friends, family, books, and nature! Keep a list of what inspires you or what makes you feel really good.

# Literal & Symbolic

So many of my clients love the beach and want to bring that feeling into their homes. Some assume that means having anchors on art and pillows and seashells all around. That's too literal! It creates a theme, which will start to feel hokey and outdated very quickly.

Instead, I help my clients go symbolic. For example, use the colors of sand and ocean, or incorporate natural textures like distressed wood. Symbolic nods toward places or things that make you happy will help you design a space you will love for many years to come. Subtlety can be powerful.

That's not to say that you can't incorporate literal representation. You might find a piece of furniture from a place you've traveled to that you want to incorporate into the overall design. Art is also a great way to do celebrate places, events, and artists you love in your space.

# Find *Your* Style

**Natural Oasis:**

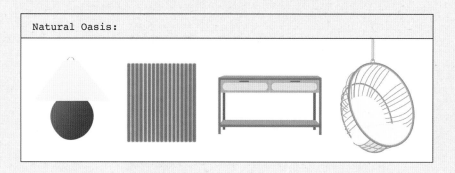

**Moody Party House:**

**Ultramodern Minimalist:**

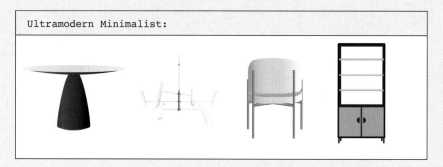

# Example Concepts

Here are some examples of concepts I've used in the past to help you see how this works.

Before you read the examples: remember that these are just examples! Use them for inspiration. Take pieces you like and combine them with other sources of inspiration. Also, look for what you don't like. You are not a category or a style created by marketers! You have your own unique concepts and your space should represent that.

## Natural Oasis

This space embraces earthy and low-key beauty. Bring in earth tones through paint and fabric. Find objects symbolic of earth, water, and sky. Look for textures and colors you find in nature. Foster a cozy, relaxed vibe with soft touches and comfy furniture.

## Moody Party House

Welcome to the party! Your design should accommodate flexible seating, so you and your guests have options of where to hang out. Pick dark colors for the walls but look for bright contrasts in textures and accents, playing with a mixture of light and dark. Use bold light fixtures and plenty of extra lamps for various lighting options. Get big, bold artwork. Use plushy textures for seating, pillows, or rugs. And don't forget the bar, which can serve as a great focal point in any living or dining space!

## Ultramodern Minimalist

I see you, clean freaks! This space is all about minimalist shapes and low-profile furniture. Invest in pieces with cabinet doors and drawers to hide clutter. Use man-made materials like glass and laminates, and balance them with natural leather for that clean, modern effect. Make sure every furniture item has a clear function, like your dining chairs. Keep the color palette neutral and bring in lots of natural light.

# A Concept That's All You

Do you believe me that I don't care what your style is? Well, here's my last rant in case you're not onboard yet.

Everyone deserves to walk into their own space and feel that "Ahhh, I'm home" feeling. The only way to reach that is to make your space feel truly your own. Sure, you can be inspired by catalogs and Instagram posts, but find out what really speaks to you.

Now that you've learned the foundations of creating a concept and read a few examples, it's time to think about your own preferences and how to incorporate them into your design. Try to think about one space at a time. Remember, you can have different concepts in different spaces!

## Fostering Feelings & Emotion

Imagine you're in your space after it has been completely redesigned. How do you want to feel? What kind of energy do you long for when you enter that space? Just like in the Function section, it's important to be honest with yourself and not try to edit based on what others think you should say or feel. Lots of people want to walk into their home and feel calm, but not everyone! Whatever is right for you is right.

Jot down the feelings you're hoping for and then try to pick two or three that best express your aspirations for the space. Here are some words to consider: calm, chill, energized, excited, focused, glamorous, hopeful, indulgent, joyful, optimistic, productive, proud, relaxed, serene, sleepy.

## Find Your Place

Think about places you have been or events you have attended where you felt your desired feelings. They can be places you've been to many times or just once, or even those you have just imagined visiting.

## Listen Carefully

What kind of music would you listen to if you wanted to feel your desired feelings? What other sounds would you choose to hear? Some popular ones are a babbling creek, white noise, or a particularly satisfying click sound.

## Dress for the Occasion

Imagine you're getting dressed just to feel your desired feelings. What would you wear? Think about the clothes you currently own or those you might want to buy just for the occasion. What would you pick?

55

Make a *Mood* Board

C33 M33 Y45 K1

# What Do You Notice?

Go through the notes you jotted down and dig just a little deeper. How are the colors, lighting, and textures related?

- In the places or events you wrote down, what colors and materials stand out to you? What do you notice about the layout of the space?

- For the sounds you named, are they sounds you prefer to hear only in certain circumstances or all the time? Do you tend to listen to those sounds over and over and then move on, or stick to them for a long time? Are these sounds something you can incorporate in your design?

- What do you notice about the clothes you would pick? Are they dark, colorful, neutral, or light? Cozy, airy, flowy, or structured? Formal or casual? Accessorized or minimalist? What do you notice about the materials you've thought about? Are they materials like natural woods, metals, or soft fabrics?

- How about your preference for color? Darker and moodier or brighter and lighter? What else stands out to you?

# Explore More!

What themes have emerged from what you've written down so far? From your notes, what will be most important to incorporate into your design?

Music is key in how my design plays out. To me, living my life is like listening to an album. Many different but similar pieces work together to create a whole. And I play it out until I've had enough. But beyond that, it's how I represent myself. I've always loved older Americana music. When I met my Palestinian fiancé, he brought Arabic music into my life. If you look around our apartment today, you'll see that it blends a modern California aesthetic with Mediterranean arches, textures, and decor.

Think about what is important to you and how to manifest it in the design of your space.

# Put It Together

Ready to name your concept? Look back through your notes at the feelings you desire; the spaces, clothes, and music that make you feel that way; and the colors, textures, materials, and pieces that will help you get there. Narrow it down by circling or starring the most important notes. And if you're really into it, pick two or three adjectives that sum it all up to give your one-of-a-kind concept its own name!

## PART 2

The Recipes

# CHAPTER FOUR

# Base Palette

I love to cook! When I was stuck at home in the early pandemic, I made elaborate meals from scratch. And what I learned from that (probably what any cook can tell you!) is that I had to know some basics before I could get to complex multi-course meals.

The same is true in design. I call it the Base Palette.

First, the Base Palette has a few foundational elements to use later for more elaborate designs. Think of the Base Palette as a base sauce or roux that you use in cooking to enhance your taste and pull the whole dish together. Without the base, you would likely have a handful of ingredients that lack flavor and cohesion.

After teaching you about some of the foundational elements of interior design (Zoning, Accessible Living, and Color Palettes), I'll dive into specifics and share the basics you need to know about Window Treatments, Wall Treatments, Lighting, Area Rugs, and Artwork & Wall Hangings. Then, for those spaces that you're just not sure what to do with, we'll address Awkward Corners, Weirdly Shaped Rooms, Weirdly Shaped Walls, and Weirdly Placed Windows.

# Zoning

It doesn't matter what sort of house you live in—be it an expansive loft, a tiny house, a cozy Craftsman, or a suburban rambler—every home benefits from functional zones. Functional zones are spaces dedicated to specific activities. The kitchen is for cooking. The bedroom is for sleeping. It seems pretty obvious, but we all have unique lifestyles and daily routines, and each space in our home needs to help—not hinder—us.

Zoning is the first step in laying the groundwork for a harmonious home. This recipe will walk you through how to assess your space and determine the different zones in your house—both existing zones and zones you'd like to create.

## What You Need:

(1) Journal or Paper (Graph Paper is Preferred)

(1) Basic Floor Plan of Your Space(s)

(1) A Pen or Pencil

01. Create the basic floor plan of your space. Draw out the space with no furniture, including only the walls and built-ins (e.g., fireplaces or cabinetry, bookshelves, and other things that cannot be moved). You can do this with graph paper and draw to scale, or use an online tool. If you choose to do it by hand, each square on your graph paper will equal one foot in real life. Keep going until you've drawn the entire space.

02. List your daily routines and activities (both good and bad ones!) that take place in your home. For instance: morning coffee, helping the kids with homework, reading in the evening, and so on. Once you've made your list, write down next to each routine or activity the corresponding spaces where they take place. For example: Feed the pups = Mudroom; Watch TV = Living room.

03. Create a bubble chart (like the one shown on the right) to help you visualize the sizes of the spaces and how they relate to each other. The size and positioning of each bubble should correlate to the size and positioning of the space. For example, if you'd like to create a reading nook in your living room, draw a smaller reading nook bubble that overlaps with the living room bubble.

04. Sketch out your rooms using your basic floor plan. Then, designate your zones—both existing zones and those you'd like to create.

05. List the furniture and other items you will need to make your zones work—this is the fun part! List out both existing pieces and those you'll need to get.

| zones | my habits |
|---|---|
| coffee bar | a dedicated space to make coffee and tea to better my morning routine |
| dining room (that extends) | dining area for 2, but can expand for additional friends and family |
| reading nook | a cozy space that I can relax and read a book in |
| open shelving wall | space to showcase my personal collections (books, records, pictures, travel memorabilia, etc.) |
| living room adult lounge | a space for the kids and a space for adults to hang out for conversation, but not formal |

## STEP ONE: LIST YOUR HABITS

Write out your daily habits, functions, and ideas for how you'd like to use the space(s). Try not to list furniture pieces; just focus on how you'll use the space.

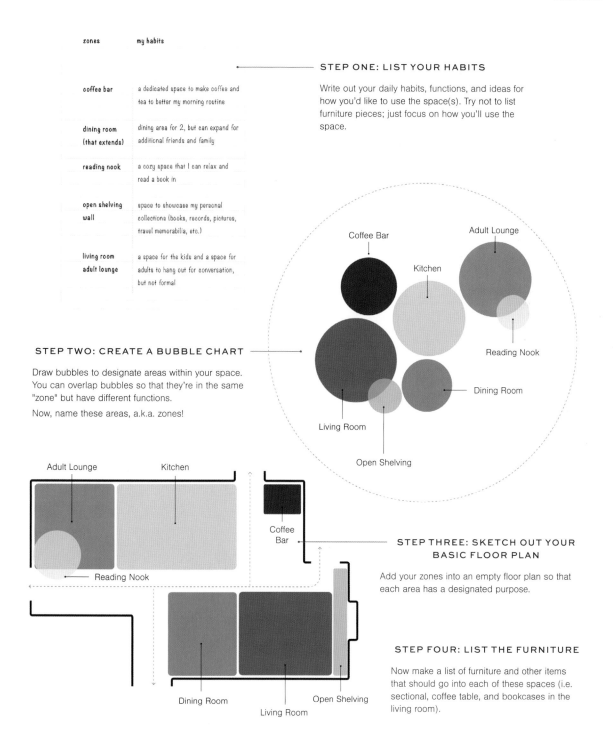

## STEP TWO: CREATE A BUBBLE CHART

Draw bubbles to designate areas within your space. You can overlap bubbles so that they're in the same "zone" but have different functions.

Now, name these areas, a.k.a. zones!

## STEP THREE: SKETCH OUT YOUR BASIC FLOOR PLAN

Add your zones into an empty floor plan so that each area has a designated purpose.

## STEP FOUR: LIST THE FURNITURE

Now make a list of furniture and other items that should go into each of these spaces (i.e. sectional, coffee table, and bookcases in the living room).

# Accessible Living

My grandmother moved in with my family when I was around six years old. When she became wheel-chair-bound a few years later, we suddenly had to think about how she'd navigate the stairs and maneuver around her bedroom that was crowded with memorabilia and little treasures. Thinking about accessibility became a part of my everyday life and I've carried that with me ever since.

In interior design, we use the term "universal design" to plan out spaces that can accommodate as many accessibility needs as possible. The recipe below shows how to apply the principles of universal design to create comfortable, functional spaces for everyone. I realize that not all of us have enough space to allow for the recommended measurements, so don't despair if you don't have enough room. Just do your best to work with the space you have.

## What You Need:

(1) Measuring Tape            (1) Basic Floor Plan of Your Space(s)

(1) A Pen or Pencil

01.  Determine the high-traffic areas in your home, such as kitchens, hallways, and entryways. Measure the existing space in those areas and record your measurements on your floor plan. Ideally, you'll try to keep at least 36–42 inches of open space in all high-traffic areas so that two people can easily pass each other as they move through the room.

02.  Determine the low-traffic areas, such as the spaces around your dining table or bed. Measure the existing space and record your measurements on your floor plan. Ideally, you'll have at least 36 inches of open space to walk through. This will offer plenty of room to move around without bumping into things or having to squeeze by.

03.  Assess your furniture placement. Can you easily reach the coffee table from the couch? Does your side table sit close enough to the arm of your easy chair? On your floor plan, note the pieces that could be rearranged to better serve your needs.

04.  Optimize. Now that you've recorded the existing measurements of your high- and low-traffic areas and furniture placement, compare your measurements to the recommended measurements. Look around to see how you can shift furniture to optimize your space and make it as functional as possible.

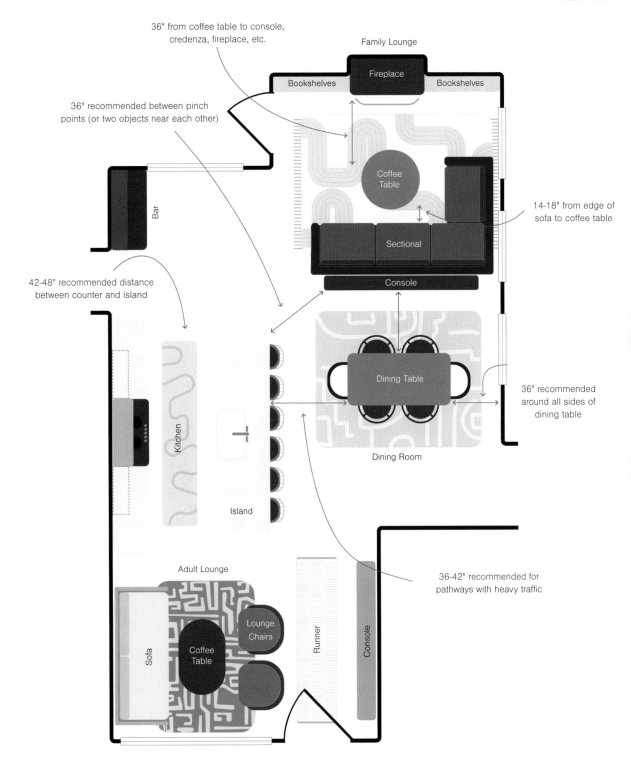

36" from coffee table to console, credenza, fireplace, etc.

Family Lounge

36" recommended between pinch points (or two objects near each other)

Bookshelves

Fireplace

Bookshelves

Coffee Table

14-18" from edge of sofa to coffee table

Bar

Sectional

Console

42-48" recommended distance between counter and island

Kitchen

Dining Table

36" recommended around all sides of dining table

Island

Dining Room

Adult Lounge

36-42" recommended for pathways with heavy traffic

Sofa

Coffee Table

Lounge Chairs

Runner

Console

# Color Palette

There's nothing that creates more harmony in a home than a cohesive color palette with complementary colors that repeat in different combinations from room to room. And I'm not just talking about wall paint here. Color palettes apply to all aspects of the home—furniture, flooring, artwork, and accessories. It's easy to get overwhelmed with all the choices, though. That's where this recipe comes in handy. It will help you narrow down color options and choose colors that bring you joy.

## What You Need:

| (1) Color Fan Deck | Inspiration Images (Optional) |
| --- | --- |

01.  Choose your palette. It can be helpful to use a color fan deck from a paint store, but if you can't get your hands on one, you can use anything for inspiration—like pages from magazines, fabric swatches, or a Pinterest board. Play around and have fun with this step. Do you find yourself drawn to cool, soothing tones? Or perhaps you love bright, contrasting colors? Look around your space. You may already have an existing color palette that you weren't aware of. Don't limit yourself here. Choose as many colors as you like. In the next step, you'll narrow down your options.

02.  Pick your base colors. Once you've determined your palette, you'll choose three base colors—the light, medium, and dark colors in your palette. I suggest you start by choosing the lightest color and work your way to the darkest. Note: the darkest color will become your accent color!

03.  Find your secondary colors. Now that you have your three base colors, you'll determine your secondary colors. Look at the medium base color you've chosen and find a color about two shades darker. Repeat this step with the darkest color, finding a color two or three shades lighter. These are your secondary colors. I recommend putting all of these color samples together (like the example shown) to have a visual of your full palette.

04.  Use the 60-30-10 ratio. You can certainly use all five colors in a room, but you don't have to. I like to focus on three colors for each room and use the main color for 60 percent of the room, the secondary color for 30 percent, and the accent color for 10 percent. For instance, in a living room, the main color could be used on the walls, the secondary color for the carpet, and the accent color for the trim or throw pillows.

▶ PRO TIP: Stuck on what colors to pick? When in doubt, think nature! Human beings crave visuals that remind them of nature. It calms us down. We can find gradients all over nature, be it in plants, desert sand, or mountain ranges! If you feel stuck, remember this: you will appreciate the colors you find in nature longer, as they are less likely to go out of style and more likely to have personal meaning to you.

# How To Create A Palette

01. Start with white or a light neutral shade.

02. Pick a medium neutral color (cream, gray, greige, etc.).

03. Pick your darkest color. This can be a neutral or an accent color—but look for the darkest you'd like to go for!

04. Pick a color 2–3 shades darker than your medium neutral.

05. Pick 2–3 shades lighter than your darkest color.

# How To Use Your Palette Like A Pro

Start with the 60-30-10 rule! 60% of the room will have your dominant color, 30% will be a secondary color, and 10% will be used as an accent for you!

60%: This is your dominant color

30%: This is your secondary color

10%: This is your accent color

# Window Treatments

Never underestimate the power of window treatments to set the mood for a room. Imagine the romantic feel of rich velvet drapes over sheer panels, or the clean, sophisticated look of crisp white Roman shades.

There are so many ways to approach window treatments, and much depends on your existing windows and particular lighting needs. For instance, think about the morning light in your bedroom—do you prefer to block it out or do you love to revel in it? And consider the windows themselves. If you have windows that open inward, then you'll need to choose a treatment that allows for this functionality.

All window treatments start with a base treatment. The page opposite shows examples of the many choices available. You can then choose to mix things up by layering different types of treatments to get the look you want.

## What You Need:

| (1) Base Window Treatment | (1) Layering Window Treatments (Optional) |
|---|---|

01.  Assess your windows to rule out any treatments that won't work for your window type. For inward-opening windows, curtains or drapes work best.

02.  Assess your lighting needs. How do you use the room? Do you rely on the window for light to read or cook by? Do you need the option to block out light so the baby can sleep?

03.  Choose your base treatment. Some options include Roman shades, wood blinds, cellular shades, curtains and drapes, roller shades, and shutters. Select one base treatment that you would be happy to use consistently throughout your home. You can customize window treatments room by room, but using the same base treatment throughout your home will provide a sense of cohesion. If you want to block out light, choose blackout shades, curtains, or wood blinds. If you want sunlight to stream in all day, choose sheer or semi-transparent curtains.

04.  Layer. If you're looking for flexibility in terms of light levels, then layer away! You can add light-blocking panels to sheer curtains or shades and close them when you're ready to darken the room. Layering also adds personality and style to a room by providing dimension and visual interest. This is where you can have some fun and make each room unique.

  ▶ PRO TIP: To give the illusion of higher ceilings and a more spacious room, mount your curtain rod as close to the ceiling as possible—typically 2–3 inches below the ceiling line or molding.

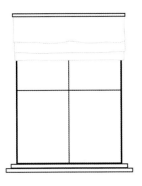

**ROMAN SHADES**

Create a sophisticated casual atmosphere

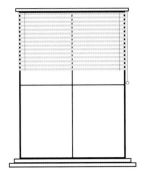

**WOOD BLINDS**

Ideal for humid location and allows more control over light levels

**CELLULAR**

Easy to maintain and allows control for both upper and lower window privacy

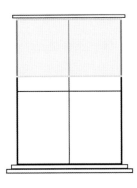

**ROLLER SHADES**

Offer a modern look for windows

**SHUTTERS**

Reduce heat and cold transfer, a classic look with a private feel

**WOVEN WOOD SHADES**

Add a natural touch while still allowing plenty of light

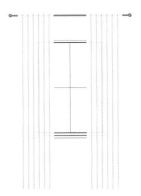

**CURTAINS OR DRAPES**

Can help reduce sound while bringing a soft touch

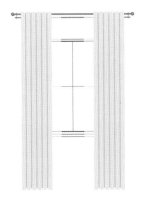

**DOUBLE LAYER CURTAINS OR DRAPES**

Can be blackout or sheer, and create a sophisticated atmosphere

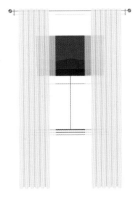

**TRIPLE LAYER TREATMENT**

Can be blackout or sheer and creates a higher-end hotel feeling

# Wall Paint

There is so much more that goes into redecorating a wall than just picking a paint color! Choosing the right type of paint finish for a room can have a drastic impact on the overall look of the space. The right paint finish can be just as fun as choosing the color, and this recipe will walk you through the best paint finishes to use throughout your home!

## What You Need:

(1) Journal of Paper

(1) Pencil or Pen

01.   Make a list of the rooms in your home that need a paint refresh and consider their usage to determine the right paint finish. Refer to the information below and at right to determine the perfect paint finish for your every room of your home.

FLAT OR MATTE PAINT: Ready to hide the imperfections? Flat or matte paint is ideal for hiding warped or damaged spots in walls or ceilings. It's great for older homes! Just keep in mind, it's not as durable as other paints—so low traffic areas are best for this finish.

EGGSHELL PAINT: You know the slight matte but also shiny shell of an egg? Well, that's eggshell paint right there! This is the most common finish we see in more modern homes. It's easy to clean and has a low reflectivity. This is best used in spaces that have moderate traffic.

SATIN PAINT: I heard you wanted all the things? Durability, cleanability, and a slight pearly look without feeling dull. Satin paint is where it's at. Satin paint can be used pretty much everywhere! It's easy to clean and patch and is ideal for high-traffic spaces.

SEMI-GLOSS PAINT: For all the clean-wall lovers, semi-gloss is where it's at. Semi-gloss paint is ideal for wet spaces, like kitchens and bathrooms—even high-traffic spaces too! This is ideal for the ease of cleaning without the intensity of high-gloss paint. Semi-gloss paint is reflective between 35 and 70 percent.

HIGH-GLOSS PAINT: Okay, risk-taker—this one's for you. High-gloss paint looks like a shellac on a wall; it has a very dramatic effect on a space. With a reflectivity of 70 percent or higher, high-gloss paint is all about the show. High-gloss paint is ideal for spaces that need extra durability or ease of cleanability.

LIMEWASH/VENETIAN PLASTER: So you want character and depth? Then lime wash is just the texture you've been dreaming of. Limewash, or venetian plaster, is one of the oldest, if not the oldest forms of color treatment to walls. The Romans and Egyptians used it! Limewash is made from limestone combined with water, then mixed together. It's mildew- and mold-resistant, making it great for wet spaces and high-traffic areas.

02.   After you've determined your paint finish, it's time to pick color. Refer to your color palette (see page 66).

**FLAT OR MATTE PAINT**

USE ME IN: Home offices or formal areas

GREAT FOR: Ceilings and low-traffic areas

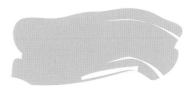

**EGGSHELL PAINT**

USE ME IN: Bedrooms, living rooms, and dining rooms

GREAT FOR: Gently-used spaces

**SATIN PAINT**

USE ME IN: Entryways, hallways, family rooms, bathrooms, and kitchens

GREAT FOR: Anywhere!

**SEMI-GLOSS PAINT**

USE ME IN: Kitchens and bathrooms

GREAT FOR: Doors, trim, and cabinets

**HIGH-GLOSS PAINT**

USE ME IN: High-traffic areas or for extreme drama

GREAT FOR: Doors, trim, cabinets, or even outdoor trim

**LIMEWASH/VENETIAN PLASTER**

USE ME IN: Any indoor or outdoor space

GREAT FOR: Any wall, bathroom, shower, or even as an outdoor treatment

# Wall Finishes

Wall paint isn't the only way you can spice up your walls! Whether you want to play up your space with different colors and patterns (hello, fun wallpaper!), or add a multidimensional look by incorporating board-and-batten, using detailed wall finishes can be a creative way to elevate your walls.

## What You Need

| | |
|---|---|
| (1) Journal of Paper | (1) Pencil or Pen |

01.  Make a list of the rooms in your home that could benefit from a wall finish refresh and refer to the information below and at right to determine the best option for every room of your home.

WALLPAPER: Wallpaper is used as a decorative element for any kind of space. It was originally used to protect walls, as wallpaper doesn't chip like paint does. It was often seen as a sign of wealth and luxury for hundreds of years.

WOOD PANELING: Wood paneling can come in all kinds of designs. The most familiar is floor to ceiling wood slat walls, beadboard, or even shiplap. It was originally used to protect walls over time, while also having a unique design element.

BOARD-AND-BATTEN: Board-and-batten is narrow pieces of wood designed in geometric patterns that typically go from floor to ceiling, or take up three-quarters of a wall. Unlike wood paneling, there are gaps between the boards, creating layers and depth on the wall.

WAINSCOTING: Wainscoting is wall paneling or tile that generally covers half of the wall to protect high-traffic areas or create visual interest on a focal-point wall.

TILE: Tile is a very durable surface that can be made of ceramic, porcelain, marble, and many more natural stones. It's used to keep things clean and water-resistant.

EXPOSED ARCHITECTURE: This finish includes brick, concrete, steel, and/or wood that is exposed as part of a design element. This is often part of the interior structure and featured for a more industrial look.

02.  After you've determined your finish, it's time to pick a color. Refer to your color palette (see page 66).

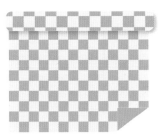

### WALLPAPER

USE ME IN: Areas of drama or visual interest

GREAT FOR: Focal points and accent walls

### WOOD PANELING

USE ME IN: Living rooms and bedrooms

GREAT FOR: Focal points and accent walls

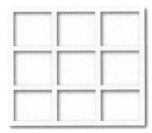

### BOARD & BATTEN

USE ME IN: Hallways, dining rooms, and any room with a focal point

GREAT FOR: Creating even taller ceilings

### WAINSCOTING

USE ME IN: Hallways, stairwells, bathrooms, and dining rooms

GREAT FOR: Protecting walls in high-traffic areas

### TILE

USE ME IN: Kitchens and bathrooms

GREAT FOR: Hot and moist climates

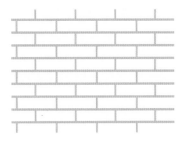

### EXPOSED ARCHITECTURE

USE ME IN: Areas of drama or visual interest

GREAT FOR: Focal points and accent walls

# Lighting

We all need a little more light in our lives, don't you think? Lighting sets the mood in a room and makes the space functional. Each room has specific needs, and there are many different lighting options available that can fulfill those needs. In a kitchen, you'll need stronger light for all your chopping, dicing, and slicing. In a bedroom, you'll want both soft, ambient light and dedicated task lighting for reading. In a playroom, you'll likely want ceiling or wall-mounted lights that your little ones can't knock over.

The beauty of lighting is that, just like color or texture, you can layer lights to create different effects. I love to use multiple types of lighting in a room. This allows you to adjust the level and type of light according to your mood or activities. This recipe outlines how to approach the different types of lighting and how to choose what's best for your particular needs.

## What You Need:

| | |
|---|---|
| (1) Journal of Paper | (1) Pencil or Pen |
| (1) Ambient Lighting | (1) Task Lighting |
| (1) Accent Lighting | |

01.  Get to know the different types of lighting. On the page opposite, you'll see three different categories of lights:

  - Ambient lighting: Overhead lights that cast light over a larger space.
  - Task lighting: Overhead lights that cast light on a specific area.
  - Accent lighting: Lamps that can be used as task lighting or to set the mood in a room.

02.  Assess your lighting needs. Think about how you use your rooms. You'll need task lighting where you do your homework, reading, or paperwork. Meanwhile, wall sconces can create a warm, cozy feel in a living room. Track lighting over a kitchen island will direct needed light onto your workspace, and a ceiling fan can provide both drama and air circulation in a dining room.

03.  Incorporate the three types of lighting. Your room will feel more complete if you use all three types of lighting in the space. It's my go-to designer secret!

**FLUSH MOUNT**

Use these with short ceilings and in hallways, kitchens, bathrooms, and closets.

**SEMI-FLUSH MOUNT**

Add character in your entryway, hall, kitchen, living room, bedrooms, bathrooms, and big closets.

**CHANDELIER**

Add drama in your dining room, living room, bedroom, large entryway, or above your stairs.

**RECESSED/CAN LIGHTS**

Use these pretty much anywhere to add lighting to a space minimally. Just remember, less is more.

**CEILING FAN**

Use a fan to create better airflow and drama in your living room and bedrooms.

**TRACK LIGHT**

Use in living rooms, hallways, kitchens, and to light artwork in a dark corner.

**STRIP LIGHTS**

Use these above or below your cabinets, on floating shelves, below your bathroom vanity, or anywhere to add a special luxurious touch.

**PENDANT**

Add function and a unique touch to your kitchen, bathroom, or above your nightstands.

**PUCK LIGHTS**

So you're renting? Use these the same way as strip lights, but with a battery—less work and a more unique look to your home.

**SCONCE**

Use these in your entryway, hallway, kitchen, living room, bedrooms, bathrooms, dining room, and big closets.

**FLOOR LAMP**

When in doubt, add a floor lamp. Add function and aesthetics to any space!

**TABLE LAMP**

Add a soft touch while adding function and a bit of character.

# Area Rugs

One of the easiest ways to add color and texture to a room is with a well-placed area rug. But you wouldn't believe how many times I've heard people say, "But I already have carpeting!" or "My kids and pets will ruin it!" There's no rule that says you can't put an area rug on top of wall-to-wall carpeting. And for those of you with messy housemates, it's easy to find washable options these days. You'll be amazed at the warmth and dimension the humble area rug can add to a space. Best of all, area rugs can be both pretty and practical.

In each recipe in this book, I'll walk through the best size of area rug to get for each type of room, but use this introductory recipe to get a feel for the basics of decorating with area rugs!

## What You Need:

(1) Measuring Tape

(1) Journal or Paper

(1) Pencil or Pen

(1) Area Rug

01. Sketch out the room or have your basic floor plan handy.

02. Measure the room and the furniture. You'll need to measure both the full size of the floor and the perimeter of the furniture bases that will sit on the rug.

03. Calculate the ideal rug dimensions for your space. I recommend keeping at least 8–12 inches between the edge of the rug and the wall, if not more. If the edge of the rug is too close to the wall, you run the risk of it overwhelming the room.

04. Choose the fiber type and pile height. For high-traffic areas such as hallways, choose a low-pile rug with tougher fibers for easier maintenance. Same for dining rooms. You'll want to ensure that you can scoot chairs in and out from the table without too much effort. For bedrooms and living rooms, higher-pile rugs lend the space a cozy, comfy feel.

05. Choose the style. Once you've determined the size, fiber type, and pile that will work best for your room, you can move on to the fun part of choosing a style. The beauty of area rugs is that you can easily change them up. So don't be shy about trying something bold to add color or texture. This works especially well when you layer rugs. You can choose a base rug style and then layer on smaller accent rugs to add visual interest. Have you always wanted a shag rug, but don't want to commit? No problem! Get a faux lambskin to throw on top of your base rug. Need some color in the bedroom? Position a vibrantly patterned rug over your base rug so it peeks out from under the bed.

    ▶ PRO TIP: Check the backing of your rug. In high-traffic areas where you don't have furniture holding the rug down, you may need a nonslip rug pad or rug tape to keep it in place. You can easily find rug pads anywhere rugs are sold, and they're a cinch to cut to size.

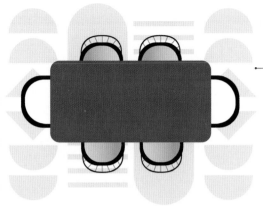

## DINING ROOM (PAGE 126)

Make sure all your chairs are fully on top of your area rug when tucked in and pulled out! Leave 24" from the edge of your table to the end of rug so you don't have any wobbly chairs.

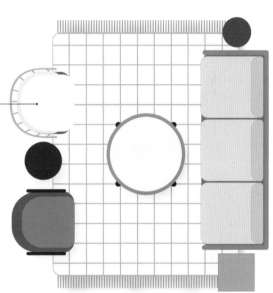

## LIVING ROOM (PAGE 102)

For cozy, intimate spaces, like bedrooms and lounges, lean into a thick, soft, or shaggy style rug. For high-traffic areas, like dining rooms, hallways, and family rooms, opt for a low-pile rug.

▶ PRO TIP: I love having washable rugs pretty much everywhere!

## BEDROOM (PAGE 166)

Try to keep at least 12–24" of flooring showing around an area rug. Yes, that can be carpet, tile, or hardwood! 18" is my personal fave!

# Artwork & Wall Hangings

Whether you're a minimalist or maximalist (or somewhere in between), how you arrange and position artwork on a wall can make or break a room. What you choose to display is entirely up to you. You might choose framed photographs, textiles, or paintings—whatever best reflects your personality and the mood you want to create. Thematic groupings are very effective to make a statement (think a wall of vintage etched mirrors or a collection of family photos). Or you might go for a bold, clean look with just a single large piece. There are no hard-and-fast rules, but there are some best practices that I'll cover in this recipe.

## What You Need:

| | |
|---|---|
| (1) Art and Wall Hangings (TVs Count!) | (1) Measuring Tape |
| (1) Journal or Paper | (1) Pencil or Pen |

01.  Measure your wall and sketch out the dimensions. Make sure to include any furniture or windows you'll be working around.

02.  Assess your space. Take note of anything that feels out of balance. Is the window off-center, extra small, or a different size than a nearby window? Do you have a tall bookshelf next to a low-profile couch?

03.  Sketch out how you'd like to arrange the artwork. This is the fun part! Get creative. You may not have all the pieces you'd like, but you can start with what you have and add to your collection over time. Here are some tips on placement:

- You don't want to fill a wall completely, but it shouldn't feel too empty either. I recommend covering about two-thirds of the visible area.
- If you're creating a grouping, but you're not sure how many pieces to feature, go with an odd number. The human eye finds harmony in odd numbers.
- Aim to keep 2–4 inches between multiple pieces of art.
- Whether you're hanging a grouping or a single piece, position the middle piece of art to match your line of vision. On average, this is about 60 inches from the floor.

▶ **PRO TIP:** If you have extra cardboard or wrapping paper lying around, cut these out to the size of your artwork to map out the wall before you hang anything!

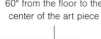

60" from the floor to the center of the art piece

4–8" above furniture pieces

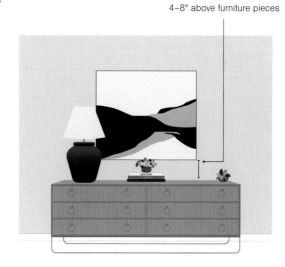

### ART ON AN EMPTY WALL

A good rule of thumb is that the center of an art piece should be about 60" above the floor—matching the average eye level and making it easier to view the piece.

### ART ABOVE A PIECE OF FURNITURE

When hanging art above furniture, leave 4–8" between the top of the furniture and the bottom of the artwork.

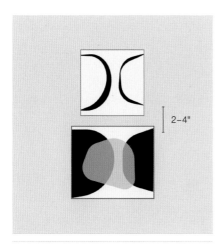

2–4"

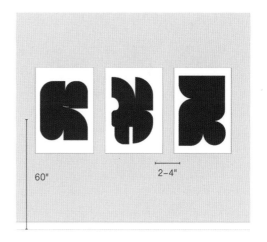

60"

2–4"

### STACKED ARTWORK

Try to keep 2–4" between art pieces.

▸ **PRO TIP:** filling two-thirds of the wall with artwork will give each piece breathing room, yet also make the wall feel full.

### TRIPTYCH ARTWORK

When in doubt, use odd numbers. It creates visual interest to the human eye.

# Awkward Corners

Many houses have areas that don't seem to serve any purpose. Most often, these spaces are found in older homes that were built when families had different needs and before the invention of central heating. That might explain the bizarre walled-off area in the bedroom that's too big to be a closet but too small to be a dressing room. Or the landing at the top of the stairs that's big enough for a chair, but not much else. These areas can provide terrific opportunities to maximize your square footage and add more comfort to your home.

For this recipe, I've shown how to take an empty corner of a larger room and make it into a reading nook. Use this as inspiration for whatever sort of space you'd like to create.

## What You Need:

(1) Measuring Tape

(1) Pencil or Pen

(1) Comfy Chair

(1) Artwork

(1) Side Table

(1) Journal or Paper

(1) Bookcase or Floating Wall Shelves

(1) Area Rug

(1) Floor Lamp or Wall-Mounted Light

01. Measure and sketch out your awkward space or have your basic floor plan handy.

02. Determine your components. Once you have the dimensions, decide which components you'll use. Ideally, you'll have space for a bookshelf, chair, floor lamp, and side table. If you don't have room for all of these elements, consider what will serve your space and needs best. Can you forego the bookshelf and find a side table that has shelving below for books? If you don't have room for a floor lamp, can you install a wall-mounted light?

03. Choose an area rug. Measure out how much space you'll need around the furniture to determine the size of the area rug you'll need.

04. Place your furniture and lighting. Lay down the rug and arrange the furniture on top. Pay special attention to the lighting. For optimal reading, you'll want to position the light so it's at shoulder height or above. See page 74 for more information on choosing lighting.

05. Accessorize. Hang your art and add a coaster on the side table for your beverage of choice. Arrange your books on the shelves and intersperse small objects around the books or create a little vignette with your favorite memorabilia. Add a cozy throw blanket and throw pillow and get to reading.

Open storage for display, frequently used objects, and things of meaning

Framed artwork for added personality

Task lighting for added focus

8" - 10" above sitting area

A purposeful place to set things down

Closed storage to keep things hidden and tucked away

An area rug to help ground the area

A place to relax and escape everday stressors

# Weirdly Shaped Rooms

Rooms come in every shape and size. You might have a really long living area that's too big for the standard couch and two chairs setup, or you might live in an old Victorian with large bay windows and pocket doors separating the front parlor into two rooms. Or you may be lucky enough to have an angled wall or wall dormers. My advice: don't fret and don't fight it! No matter how oddly your room is shaped, you can use its shape to your advantage. In this recipe I show how to make the most of an angled wall and a long living room, but you can apply the principles to any sort of space.

## What You Need

(1) Measuring Tape

(1) Journal or Paper

(1) Pencil or Pen

01. Sketch out your space or refer to your basic floor plan. Identify the oddity. What makes the room a challenge?

02. Embrace and optimize the oddity. In the case of an angled wall, consider making it an accent wall or a focal point by hanging a dramatic piece of art on it. In the case of a long room, think about how you can create multiple zones within the room. Refer to the zoning recipe on page 62 for tips on designating multiple functional spaces within a single room.

03. Think about traffic. When figuring out where to place furniture, consider the doorways and pathways between furniture. Make sure you leave space for people to easily get from point A to point B. The Accessible Living recipe on page 64 offers ideal measurements for throughways.

04. Counterbalance. Use shapes that offset the awkwardness. In the diagram of the room with the angled wall, you'll see I've used circular and oval shapes to counter the slant of the wall. In the diagram of the extra-long room, I placed a console table behind the sofa to create distinct zones between the lounge area, traffic lane, and reading nook.

Break up angled and straight lines with organic shapes, circles, and soft lines. Contrast is what will make this space feel cohesive and finished.

This wall has become the focal point; all furniture in the room facing this way will address the weird angle.

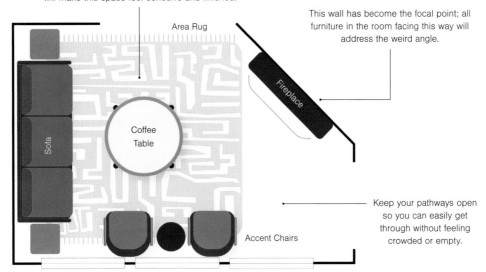

Keep your pathways open so you can easily get through without feeling crowded or empty.

## ROOMS WITH ODDLY-ANGLED WALLS

Avoid angling furniture towards an angled wall—it will create dead corners and useless space behind the furniture.

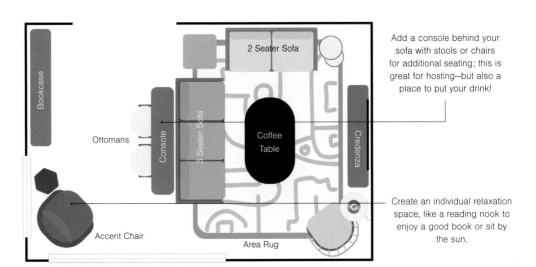

Add a console behind your sofa with stools or chairs for additional seating; this is great for hosting—but also a place to put your drink!

Create an individual relaxation space, like a reading nook to enjoy a good book or sit by the sun.

## LONG ROOMS WITH MULTIPLE PURPOSES

Zone this area as a designated lounge! This will help break up a large room without making it feel disjointed. This is great for transitioning from everyday life into entertainment hours.

# Weirdly Shaped Walls

Most of us have experienced the awkwardness of weirdly shaped walls. Whether it's at an angle or has vaulted ceilings that cut the wall short, half the battle of decorating an oddly shaped wall is understanding how you can make it a focal point. Rather than trying to ignore it, try to add elements that will draw your eye towards it. Don't fret the oddly shaped wall; learn to embrace it and work with it. Be unique.

## What You Need

| | |
|---|---|
| (1) Journal or Paper | (1) Pencil or Pen |
| (1) Painter's Tape | (1) Artwork |
| (1) Mirror | (1) Floor Lamp, Table Lamp, and/or Sconce |
| (1) Picture Rails | (1) Sofa |
| (1-2) Accent Chair(s) | (1) Side Table(s) |

01. Head back to geometry class. Start by thinking of the wall as a shape. If the wall is a triangle, what would you do to draw your eye up to the tip of the triangle? Remember: we're embracing the odd shape of the wall, not trying to conceal it!

    If the wall is an asymmetrical shape (like illustrations A and B) you would draw a line from the lowest point of the wall to the tallest point.

    If the wall's shape is impacted by a vaulted ceiling (as shown in illustrations C and D), draw a line from the center of the point downward. Your focal point should be in the center of the shape, and this draws your eye inwards.

02. Pull out a roll of painter's tape. Depending on your wall's shape, recreate the corresponding line on your wall using painter's tape. Working from the shortest part of the wall to the tallest part, tape out the line from edge to edge. That's the line we'll follow to draw your eye upward and make this weird wall the favorite wall in your home.

03. Follow the line. Now, trace the line with objects! We'll use things like artwork, mirrors, or picture rails to draw our eye upward and along the line. You just used the power of sacred geometry, and you didn't even know it! This method will address the shape of the wall, work with it, and make the space feel complete. The goal of this is to make the wall look larger than life.

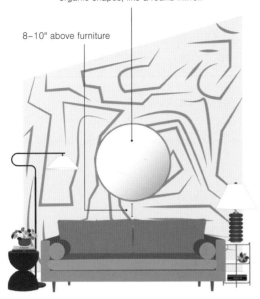

Break up the angled lines with organic shapes, like a round mirror.

8–10" above furniture

## SUBTLE ASYMMETRICAL-ANGLED WALL

Create balance with a tall lamp on the short side of the angled wall.

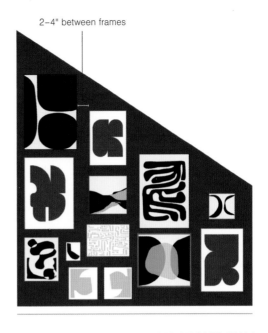

2–4" between frames

## STEEP ASYMMETRICAL-ANGLED WALL

Give the illusion of height, depth, and completion by following the angle upward. Stack oversized atwork to fill the entire space.

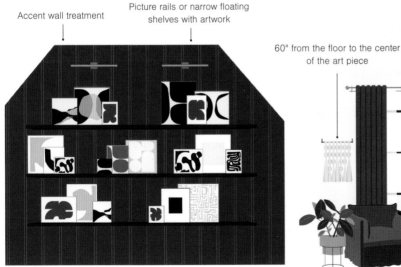

Accent wall treatment

Picture rails or narrow floating shelves with artwork

60" from the floor to the center of the art piece

Hang rod 8–10" above window trim

## A FLAT VAULT

16–20" between each shelf for artwork

## SYMMETRICAL VAULTS

Asymmetrical elements can be used to contrast a symmetrical vaulted ceiling. Try a large sconce in contrast to a wall tapestry or art piece.

# Weirdly Placed Windows

If you happen to have an oddly placed window, don't despair. Some of the most striking rooms are those with something a bit off-kilter. The secret is to work with the window, not against it. This recipe offers ideas on how to work with what your room has to offer and use window treatments, art, accessories, or lighting fixtures to create balance. Look at it as an opportunity to get creative!

## What You Need

| | |
|---|---|
| (1) Measuring Tape | (1) Journal or Paper |
| (1) Pencil or Pen | Stacked Art Pieces (Two or More Recommended) |
| (1) Dimensions of Existing or Desired Furniture | Window Treatments |
| Room Dimensions | Plants |
| Light Fixtures | Accessories |

01. Sketch out the room or use your basic floor plan to get a clear picture of the window placement and room dimensions. What's off-balance? Is the window off-center, extra small, or a different size than a nearby window?

02. Assess your options. Consider the resources you have and what's possible in your space. For instance, if you can't drill holes in the walls, you'll need to rule out a wall-mounted light, but you could consider a standing lamp or tall plant to balance things out.

03. Play. Using the sketch of your room or your basic floor plan, play around with what might work to create balance and harmony. Here's a brief reference guide to get your creative juices flowing:

    • Framed art can give the illusion of a second window. Try stacking or arranging multiple pieces to mirror the shape and size of the oddly placed window.
    • Position an oversized light or tall plant to create balance.
    • Hang long curtains or extend curtain rods over multiple windows to give the feeling of a larger window.
    • A bookshelf or console with thoughtfully chosen accessories can complement an oddly placed window and create visual balance.

20" between top of nightstand to light

## BALANCE WITH LIGHT

Balance an offset window with an oversized light fixture on the opposite side. This will even out the space and call attention to the light over your awkward window.

2–4" between artwork

## TRICK YOUR EYE WITH ART

Stack two pieces of art on top of each other to mimic the window on the other side of the wall. Try layering lighting and/or plants with this to create visual interest.

▶ PRO TIP: The frames don't have to be the exact same height or width as the window on the opposite side of the wall!

## MAKE SMALL WINDOWS FEEL LARGER

If your windows are small or are hidden behind furniture, give the illusion that your entire wall is a window. Hang curtains directly from the ceiling with a hidden rod and the whole space will instantly feel enlarged!

# CHAPTER FIVE

# Entryways

The entryway may seem like a pretty straightforward space, but we ask a lot of this humble space. We want it to feel warm and inviting, but we also want it to do the hard work of keeping our lives in order.

Whether you have an open and airy entry or a small vestibule, the recipes in this section will show you how to make the space work for your specific needs. The first step is to think about function and your personal routines. Don't worry, we'll get to making the space beautiful, too! But don't forget what you learned earlier in this book—the way to create and maintain beautiful spaces is to design around. . . you guessed it—your specific habits! If you need a refresher, refer back to the Function chapter on page 14 to help you think through your particular habits and needs.

In this section, we'll first go over the key components of an entryway and then I'll offer up recipes to treat different types of spaces and different functional needs. The first recipe shows a basic entryway with the essential pieces in place. The rest of the recipes treat specific spaces. Take what you need from each recipe to create your own warm, inviting, and hardworking entry.

With each recipe you'll find floor plans to give you multiple examples on how to arrange furniture in your space. Reference the numbered list below to identify what goes where.

## Furniture List:

| | | |
|---|---|---|
| 1. Area Rug | 14. Dresser | 27. Round Entry Table |
| 2. Basket | 15. Fireplace | 28. Sectional |
| 3. Bench | 16. Floor Lamp | 29. Shoe Cabinet |
| 4. Bookshelf/Tall Cabinet | 17. Freestanding Tub | 30. Shower |
| 5. Cabinets | 18. Island | 31. Side Table |
| 6. Coffee Table | 19. King Bed | 32. Sink |
| 7. Console | 20. Lounge Chair | 33. Sofa |
| 8. Counter/Bar Stools | 21. Nightstand | 34. Toilet |
| 9. Credenza | 22. Ottoman | 35. Tub/Shower |
| 10. Desk | 23. Planter | 36. Twin Bed |
| 11. Desk Chair | 24. Queen Bed | 37. Vanity |
| 12. Dining Chair | 25. Range | 38. Crib |
| 13. Dining Table | 26. Refrigerator | |

# Medium / Large Entryway

This recipe shows how to create a fully functional and beautiful entryway. Your entryway may not be this size or shape, but you can use this as a template and apply the principles to your own particular space.

## What You Need:

(1) Console: 60" W x 18" D

(1) Mirror: 36" Round

(1) Flush Mount or Semi-Flush Mount Light

(1) Runner: 72" L x 30" W (or Rug: 4' x 6')

(3–6) Wall Hooks

## Add-Ons:

(1) Ottoman: 18" Diameter

(1) Bowl or Tray

(1) Small Plant

(1) Tall Basket with a Lid

(1) Mail Pouch

01. Assess your routines and habits. Refer back to the Function chapter (page 14) to make sure you've listed out all of your specific needs.

02. Organize. Choose elements that are both practical and pleasing to the eye. An open console with a couple of drawers does double duty of providing surface area to set things down and drawers to tuck clutter away. A tall basket with a lid provides a handy place to stow larger items, such as bike helmets or umbrellas. A storage ottoman gives you a spot to sit down and put on your shoes and room to store things out of sight until you need them again. Wall hooks are perfect for hats, scarves, and other smaller items that could easily get lost in a storage basket or ottoman. Handy for stashing mail you want to get to later, a mail slot keeps snail mail from piling up and taking over surfaces.

03. Light it up. It's easy to overlook lighting in an entryway if the space gets plenty of sunlight during the day. But the right kind of light can create a distinct feeling of warmth and welcome. I recommend flush mount lighting for ambient light. Add a mirror to reflect the light and make the entryway feel even bigger. A mirror also gives you one last chance to check yourself out on the way out the door.

04. Watch your step. Choose a rug made from a durable fiber to wipe your feet. Make sure to choose a rug with nonslip backing or pair it with a nonslip pad.

05. Accessorize. Look for accessories that both complement your space and serve a function. A handsome bowl makes a lovely style statement and provides a spot to put your small items.

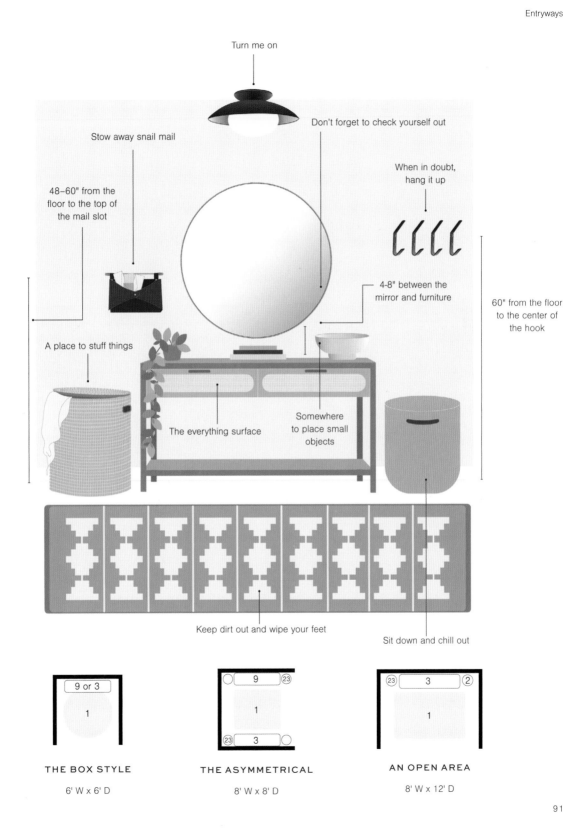

Turn me on

Don't forget to check yourself out

Stow away snail mail

When in doubt, hang it up

48–60" from the floor to the top of the mail slot

60" from the floor to the center of the hook

4-8" between the mirror and furniture

A place to stuff things

Somewhere to place small objects

The everything surface

Keep dirt out and wipe your feet

Sit down and chill out

**THE BOX STYLE**

6' W x 6' D

**THE ASYMMETRICAL**

8' W x 8' D

**AN OPEN AREA**

8' W x 12' D

# Small Entryway

Live in a small apartment or tiny home? Then this recipe is for you. I live in a 600-square-foot apartment and believe me, I know how hard it is to stay tidy in such cramped quarters. I'm here to tell you that it's possible to create a fully functioning, gorgeous entryway with minimal space. This recipe treats two types of small entryways: a narrow hallway, and a wall next to the front door that's been zoned to act as an entryway.

## What You Need:

| | |
|---|---|
| (1) Console: 48" W x 12" D | (1) Floating Shelf |
| (1) Mirror: 36" Round | (1) Flush Mount or Semi-Flush Mount Light |
| (1) Runner: 72" L x 30" W | (3–6) Wall Hooks |

01. Assess your routines and habits. Refer back to the Function chapter (page 14) to make sure you've listed out all of your specific needs.

02. Organize. In small spaces, it's especially important to keep things organized. You'll need to keep the components minimal to fit your small space:

    CONSOLE: For the narrow hallway entry, I chose a narrow console with cabinets. It provides a bit of surface area to set things down on and the cabinets provide extra storage space. For the one-wall entryway, I recommend a wall-mounted floating shelf to provide some storage while taking up minimal space and helping the space feel light and airy.

    STORAGE OTTOMAN: For the one-wall entry, tucking ottomans under the floating shelf provides both storage and a spot to sit down to put your shoes on.

    HOOKS: Wall hooks are perfect for hats, scarves, and other smaller items that could easily get lost in the storage basket or ottoman. Arrange the hooks in a way that makes the most sense for the space, but be mindful of allowing enough room between the hooks and whatever sits beneath so you don't end up with a jumbled mess.

03. Light it up. In both of these examples, I used flush mount lights to lend an "Ooh! Welcome home!" feel. If your hallway is long enough, you can install a series of semi-flush mount lights along the way. And don't forget the mirror to reflect light and create the illusion of even more space.

04. Watch your step. Choose a small rug or runner made from a durable fiber to wipe your feet. It's best to choose a low-pile option with nonslip backing or pair the rug with a nonslip pad.

05. Accessorize. In the one-wall entry, I used a small bowl to hold keys and other small items. Next to the bowl I added a small houseplant with trailing leaves and a tall, narrow vase for visual interest. Neither takes up too much space and they balance out the other elements.

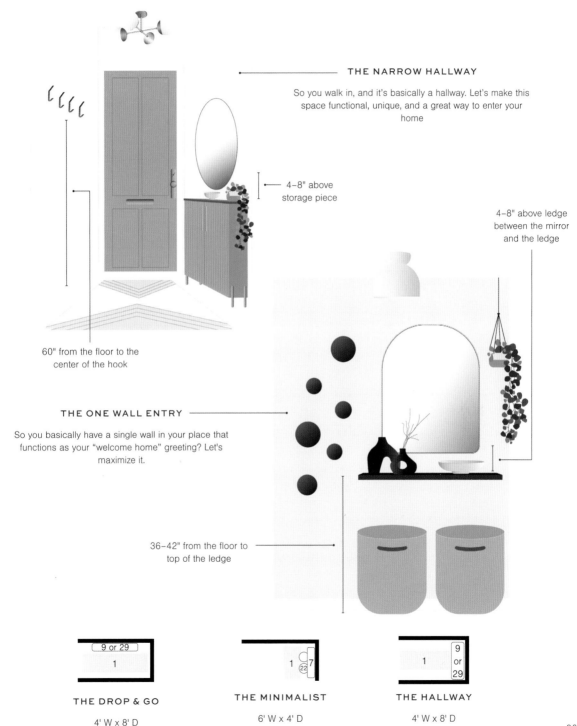

## THE NARROW HALLWAY

So you walk in, and it's basically a hallway. Let's make this space functional, unique, and a great way to enter your home

4–8" above
storage piece

4–8" above ledge
between the mirror
and the ledge

60" from the floor to the
center of the hook

## THE ONE WALL ENTRY

So you basically have a single wall in your place that functions as your "welcome home" greeting? Let's maximize it.

36–42" from the floor to
top of the ledge

9 or 29
1

**THE DROP & GO**

4' W x 8' D

1  7
22

**THE MINIMALIST**

6' W x 4' D

1
9
or
29

**THE HALLWAY**

4' W x 8' D

# Grand Entryway

Can there be such a thing as too much space? A grand entryway can be tricky to deal with because you want it to feel functional and welcoming, yet still dramatic and not too formal. Managing all of this is a tall order, I know, but the recipe below will show you how to put the pieces in place.

## What You Need:

(1) Console: 60" W x 20" D

(1) Round Table: 48" Round

(1) Rug: 8' Round

(1) Bench: 60" W x 18" D

(1) Chandelier

(1–2) Ottoman(s) 18" Diameter

## Add-Ons:

(1) Large Vase

(1) Small Plant

(2) Pillows

(1) Medium Plant

(1) Bowl or Tray

01. Assess your routines and habits. Refer back to the Function chapter (page 14) to make sure you've listed out all of your specific needs.

02. Organize. This space is too gorgeous for clutter. I chose a console with cabinets to hide shoes, packages, keys, and other items that can easily accumulate in an entryway. A storage ottoman set below the entry table provides a spot to sit and put on your shoes before you run out the door.

03. Light it up. In a grand entryway, it's all about the drama. I used an oversized chandelier to make a bold, dramatic statement.

04. Make space for guests. In this big, grand space, make sure guests feel welcome by providing creature comforts. A bench offers a spot to take off shoes and rest for a moment, while the entry table with the storage ottoman underneath provides another area to sit and get organized.

05. Watch your step. The rug I chose echoes the shape of the entry table. It's low-pile, but because it sits beneath a table rather than a main traffic-way, I didn't have to worry about durability and chose a soft wool.

06. Accessorize. The chandelier is the star of the show, so I kept the rest of the accessories low-key. I propped two small pillows on the bench; placed a vase with sinuous lines on the round tabletop; and set a bowl, a catch-all tray, and a small potted plant on the console.

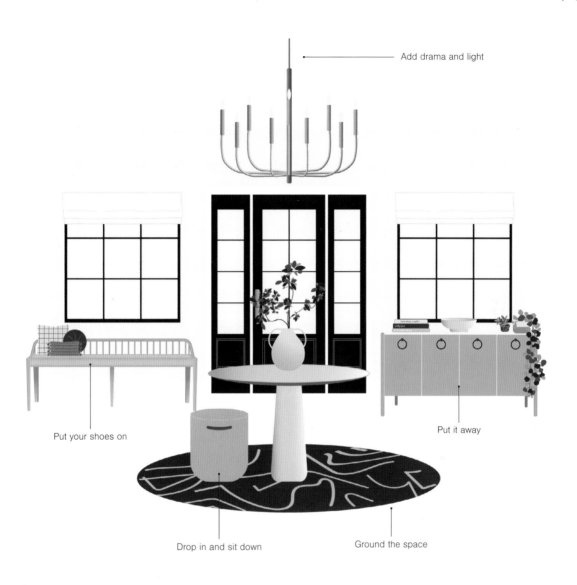

Add drama and light

Put your shoes on

Put it away

Drop in and sit down

Ground the space

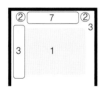

**THE DROP & GO**

10' W x 12' D

**BEHIND THE SOFA**

10' W x 15' D

**SIT DOWN & RELAX**

15' W x 20' D

# Staircase Entryway

What I love about a staircase entryway is the height and drama of the space. You may not have much floor space to work with, but that's okay. You'll be amazed at what you can do with a few well-placed pieces.

## What You Need:

(1) Console: 48–60" W x 20" D

(1) Round Table: 30" Round

(1) Runner: 6–8' L x 2'6" W

## Add-Ons:

(1) 30" Mirror

(1) Large Vase

(1) Small Plant

(1) Bowl or Tray

01. Assess your routines and habits. Refer back to the Function chapter (page 14) to make sure you've listed out all of your specific needs.

02. Organize. The trick to a functional, welcoming entryway with a staircase is to choose components that are in proportion to the wall space.

    CONSOLE: I chose an open console with a slim profile. The drawers and baskets beneath provide a place to tuck clutter away. There's just enough room on the top for a few accessories that are both pretty and practical.

    ROUND TABLE: A small round table is a great option if your space is narrow. This table's clean lines echo the clean lines of the stair railing and windows.

03. Light it up. Overhead ambient lighting works best in a staircase entryway. I recommend flush mount lighting to cast light over the entire space.

04. Watch your step. Staircase entryways generally don't have much floor space, so you'll likely need to look for a larger doormat or short runner. Choose one made from a durable fiber with nonslip backing or pair it with a nonslip pad or rug tape.

05. Accessorize. A mirror does wonders in creating the illusion of more space and light. Look for one that will fit tidily on the diagonal wall space. If you choose a round table for your entry, then I recommend a medium-sized vase placed in the center of the tabletop. You can change out the flowers or branches whenever you're looking for a refresh. A small bowl and tray makes a lovely style statement.

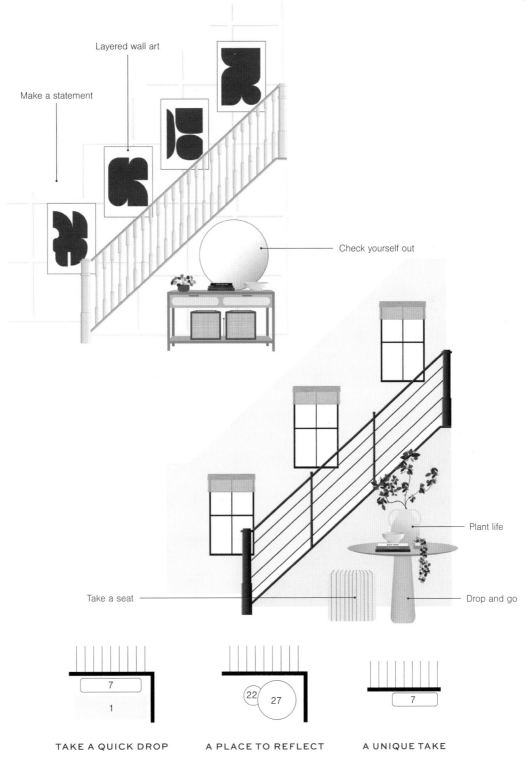

Make a statement

Layered wall art

Check yourself out

Plant life

Take a seat

Drop and go

**TAKE A QUICK DROP**

4–6' long

**A PLACE TO REFLECT**

6' x 3' long

**A UNIQUE TAKE**

6' x 3' long

# Open-Concept Entryway

No entryway? No problem. We'll hack one! Here's where zoning comes into play (see page 62). I've provided options here for three different solutions: a drop station against a wall, a sofa console (if your sofa faces away from the door), or a bench. Pick the one that works best for your space or mix and match!

## What You Need:

| Drop Station | Behind Your Sofa | Relax & Take a Seat |
|---|---|---|
| (1) Console: 48" W x 12" D | (1) Console: 60–72" W x 12" D | (1) Bench: 60" W x 18" D |
| (1) Mirror: 36" Round | (1) Runner: 72" L x 30" W | (1) Runner: 72" L x 30" W |
| (1) Semi-Flush Mount | | (1) Semi-Flush Mount |
| (1) Runner: 72" L x 30" W | | |
| (1) Coat-tree | | |

## Add-Ons:

| | | |
|---|---|---|
| (1) Ottoman: 18" Diameter | (1) Semi-Flush Mount | (4) Wall Hooks |
| (1-2) Tall Basket(s) with a Lid | (2) Pillows | (1) Bowl or Tray |
| (1) Mail Pouch | | |

01.  Assess your routines and habits. What do you need most? Determine if you need space to hang things, change shoes, or drop everything off. If your front door opens into an open-concept room, try to choose items that serve double duty, like the sofa console which also gives you space to set drinks down. Refer back to the Function chapter (page 14) to make sure you've listed out all of your specific needs and refer to the Zoning section (page 62) for a refresher on how to create zones within a room.

02.  Organize. Once you've determined what sort of entryway you'll create, you'll choose your core components.

## CREATE A DROP STATION

Utilize a wall when you walk in for the drop-and-go: a place to put keys, bags, sweaters, and more as soon as you get home.

4" - 8" above console

non stop reader

**DROP STATION**

3–5' long

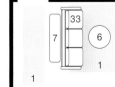

**BEHIND YOUR SOFA**

5–8' long

**RELAX & TAKE A SEAT**

4–7' long

**DROP STATION**: For a drop station, it's all about easy access and minimal space.

- Console: This console has a sleek, minimal profile. You can stash mail, hats, and gloves in the drawers and the open shelf below acts as the perfect spot to store your shoes.
- Coat-tree: This coat-tree takes up very little room with its short "branches." Bonus: you won't have to drill holes into the wall for hooks, making coat-trees ideal for renters.

**BEHIND YOUR SOFA**: With a little creativity, you can turn the empty space behind your couch into a handsome and welcoming entryway area.

- Console: I chose an open console that does double duty—you can use the top for items like mail and keys, and you can set your drink on it when you're kicking up your feet after a long day.
- Storage baskets: I used the open space under the console shelf to tuck two open-top storage baskets, which make handy catchalls.
- Open shoe storage: If you have a shoes-off household, then a handsome shoe rack makes for a tidy solution. No more piles of shoes in a jumble on the floor!
- Hooks: Guests can easily hang their items and not forget them when they leave!

**RELAX & TAKE A SEAT**: I love the versatility of a bench in open-concept entryways. It's always nice to have a spot to sit and take off your shoes and rifle through the mail.

- Bench: I chose a bench with space for storage underneath. It's lightweight and you can easily move it around to provide additional seating for guests.
- Storage baskets: Two open-top storage baskets slide under the bench and provide ample space for your gear.
- Hooks: Perfect for hats, scarves, and other smaller items that could easily get lost in the storage baskets. I arranged these hooks low enough to easily reach yet high enough to leave space for you to sit on the bench.

03. Light it up. Because you're creating an entryway zone within a room that serves a larger purpose, you may not have much flexibility here. In the Relax & Take a Seat example, I use a semi-flush mount light because it helps define the space.

04. Accessorize: You'll likely need to keep accessories to a minimum, so choose items that are both stylish and functional.

**DROP STATION**: I placed a tray in the center of the console top and set a small potted plant on one side and a sleek bowl on the other side to stash keys, spare change, or mail.

**BEHIND YOUR SOFA**: The wide-mouth bowl and tray on the top of console provide stylish receptacles for mail and keys. I chose a small plant with a low profile to avoid the risk of greenery from a taller plant tickling the back of a person's neck while they sit on the sofa.

**RELAX & TAKE A SEAT**: To add a soft touch to the bench, I chose a rectangular and square pillow that are rather flat so they don't take up too much space.

### UTILIZE THE BACK OF YOUR SOFA

By making use of the unusable space behind your sofa, you can create a great drop station and an excellent place to put your drink when watching TV or visiting with friends.

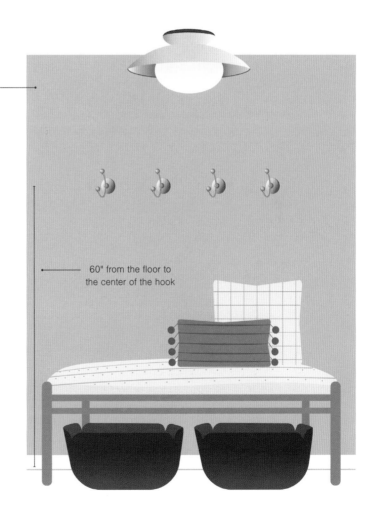

### RELAX & TAKE A SEAT

A bench offers an easy place to relax and a great way to add hidden storage. Install hooks on the wall to store smaller items, like hats and scarves!

60" from the floor to the center of the hook

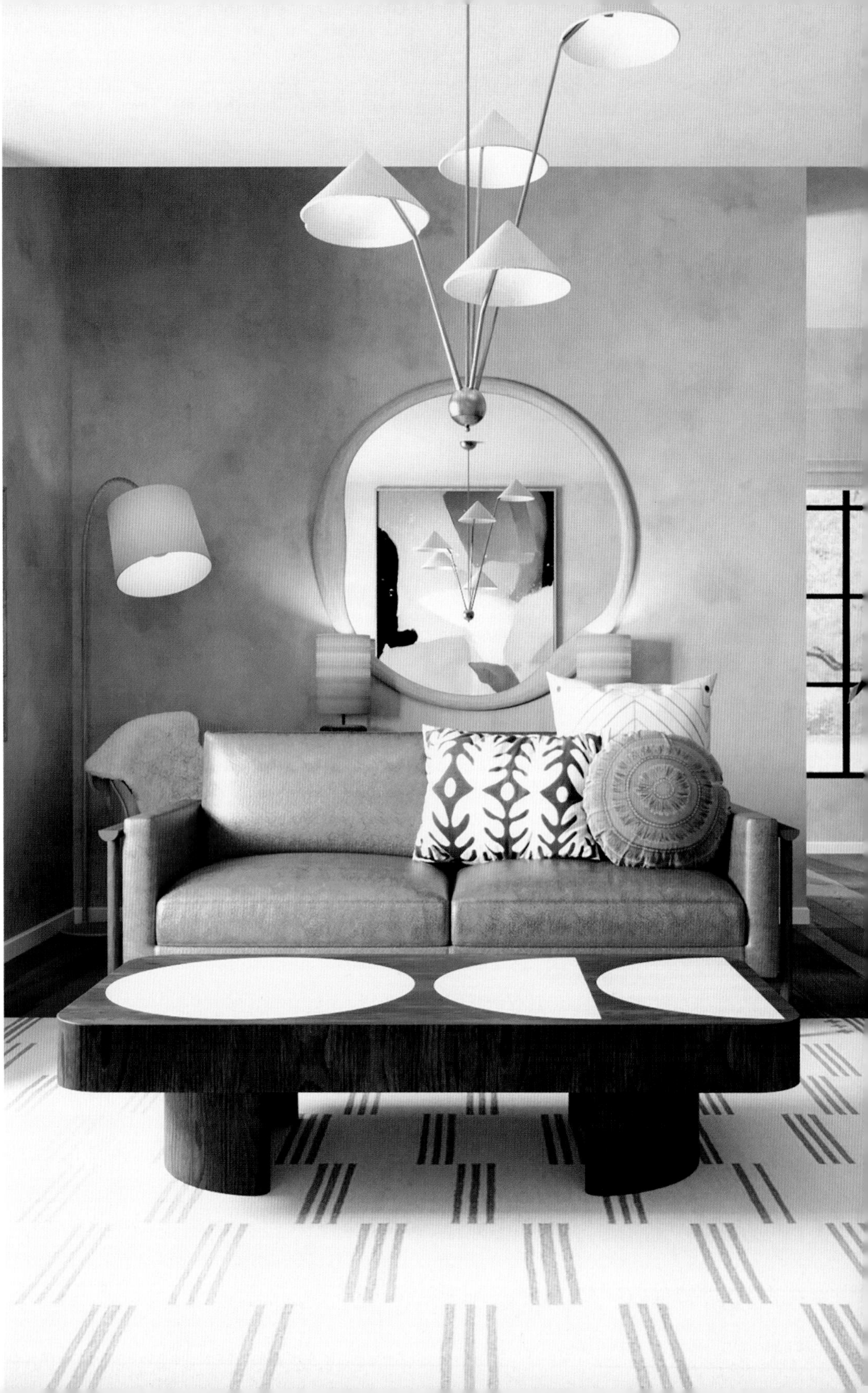

# CHAPTER SIX

# Living Room

Living room, front room, family room, den . . . whatever you call it, this is the room where we gather to relax and celebrate. Gone are the days of "formal" living rooms. Remember those fancy rooms that your mom forbade you to go into for fear you'd make a mess or break something? Such a waste of space! The recipes in this section are for living rooms that are meant to be lived in.

# Tiny Living Room

I have a soft spot for the tiny apartment—living in 600 square feet will do that! And I'm here to tell you that it's absolutely possible to create a gorgeous, fully functional living room in a very small space. The trick is to maximize every inch. This recipe offers three different configurations in the same-size space.

## What You Need:

| Simple & Cozy<br>7' W x 10' D | Cozy, Cozy, Cozy<br>7' W x 10' D | A Special Space<br>7' W x 10' D |
|---|---|---|
| (1) Sofa: 72" W | (1) Sofa: 72" W | (1) Sofa: 72" W |
| (1) Credenza: 60" W x 12" D | (1) Media Console: 60" x 20" | (1) Console: 60" L x 20" D |
| (1) Floating Shelf: 48" L x 6" D | (1) Sofa Console: 60-72" x 12" | (1) Floating Shelf: 48" L x 6" D |
| (1) Semi-Flush Mount | (1) Semi-Flush Mount | (1) Credenza: 72" W x 20" D |
| (2) Side Tables: 20" x 20" | (1) Coffee Table: 30" Diameter | (1) Semi-Flush Mount |
| (1) Ottoman: 18–20" Diameter | (1) Area Rug: 6' Round | (2) Ottomans: 18–20" Diameter |
| (1) Area Rug: 5' x 8' | (1) TV: 43–50" | (2) Area Rugs: 3' x 5' |
| (1) TV: 43–50" | | (1) TV: 43–50" |

## Add-Ons:

| | | |
|---|---|---|
| (1) Plug-in Wall Sconce | (1) Floating Shelf: 48" L x 6" D | (4) Wall Hooks |
| (1) Table Lamp | (1) 16" W x 20" H Frame | (2) Baskets |
| (1) Floor Lamp | (2) Pillows | |

01.  Assess your space. Refer to your floor plan or sketch things out if that's helpful. Your sketch doesn't have to be perfect, and it will help you envision which elements will work for your particular space.

02.  Choose your core components. Refer to page 125 for tips on choosing the perfect sofa and coffee table combo.

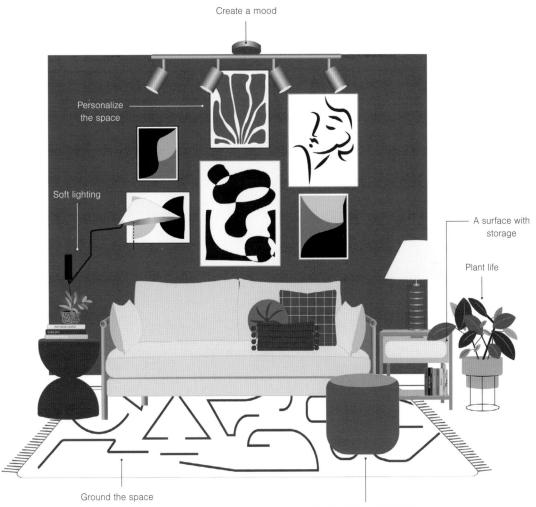

Create a mood

Personalize the space

Soft lighting

A surface with storage

Plant life

Ground the space

Put your feet up or sit down

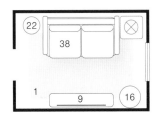

**SIMPLE & COZY**

7' W x 10' D

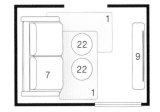

**COZY, COZY, COZY**

7' W x 10' D

**A SPECIAL SPACE**

7' W x 10' D

03. Organize! In small spaces, the secret to success is to find as many ways as possible to incorporate storage. In the "Simple & Cozy" room shown opposite, the side table, ottoman, open basket, closed console, and floating shelves all provide areas to store items, either out in the open or hidden away.

04. Light it up. In this living room, I used four different types of lighting fixtures—which may seem like a lot for a small space, but each fixture has a specific job. The overhead track lighting provides overall illumination. On one side of the couch, I used a table lamp with a narrow base. On the other side, I freed up the side table surface area by installing a wall-mounted adjustable light. The standing lamp next to the TV provides height next to the large screen and floating shelf.

05. Watch your step. I positioned a large rectangular rug so it extends out from beneath the couch to provide lots of room to lounge on the floor with pillows while you watch TV. I like medium-pile rugs for these spaces because of their softness. Because this isn't a high-traffic area, you don't have to worry so much about durability.

06. Accessorize. In a small space, it's best to keep the number of accessories to a minimum, but that's no reason to skimp on style. In small spaces, I like to make the most of the wall by arranging six different-sized pieces of artwork above the couch and adding a few small plants on the console, the floating shelf, and next to the side table. The pillows on the couch add color and softness, and you can tuck extra pillows and throw blankets in the storage ottoman.

Accentuate your memories and treasures

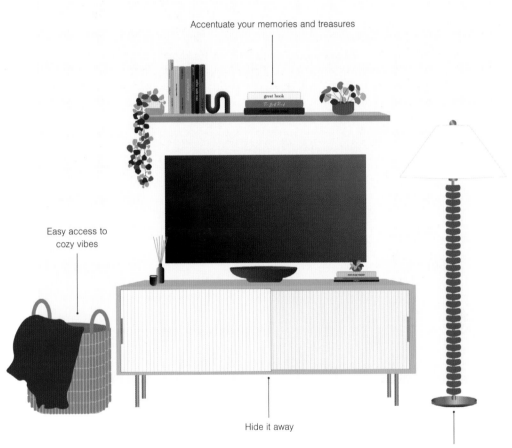

Easy access to
cozy vibes

Hide it away

Create height and light it up

# Small Living Room

So, your living room isn't exactly tiny, but it doesn't have tons of space either? I'll show you how to maximize your room without overcrowding it. This recipe offers three different configurations in the same-size space. Follow one ingredient list or mix and match to tailor the recipe to meet your needs.

## What You Need:

| Spatial Balance<br>10' W x 13' D | Meant for Lounging<br>10' W x 13' D | Unique & Thoughtful<br>10' W x 13' D |
|---|---|---|
| (1) Sofa: 72" W | (1) Sectional: 96" W x 72" L | (1) Sofa: 96" W |
| (1) Coffee Table: 42" L x 24" W | (1) Coffee Table: 30" Diameter | (1) Coffee Table: 30" Diameter |
| 1) Side Table: 20" x 20" | (1) Desk: 48" W x 24" D | (1) Console: 72" W x 12" D |
| (1) Accent Chair | (1) Desk Chair | (1) Accent Chair |
| (1) Credenza: 72" W x 20" D | (1) Accent Chair | (1) Credenza: 72" W x 20" D |
| (1) Semi-Flush Mount | (1) Credenza: 72" W x 20" D | (1) Semi-Flush Mount |
| (1) Area Rug: 8' x 10' | (1) Semi-Flush Mount | (1) Area Rug: 6' x 9' |
| (1) TV: 55–65" | (1) Area Rug: 8' x 10' | (1) TV: 55–65" |
|  | (1) TV: 55–65" |  |

## Add-Ons:

| | | |
|---|---|---|
| (1) Plug-in Wall Sconce | (1) Table Lamp | (1) Floor Lamp |
| (1) Floating Shelf: 48" L x 6" D | | |

01. Assess your space. Refer to your floor plan or sketch things out if that's helpful. Your sketch doesn't have to be perfect, and it will help you envision which elements will work for your particular space.

02. Choose your core components. Refer to page 125 for tips on choosing the perfect sofa and coffee table combo. In the "Meant for Lounging" living room shown opposite, I chose a sofa with a built-in chaise and paired it with a round coffee table that fits the space in front of the other half of the couch.

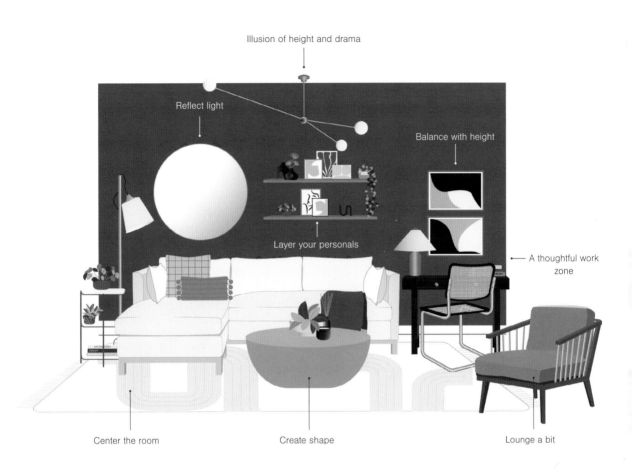

Illusion of height and drama

Reflect light

Balance with height

Layer your personals

A thoughtful work zone

Center the room

Create shape

Lounge a bit

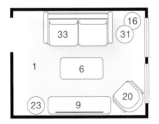

**SPATIAL BALANCE**

10' W x 13' D

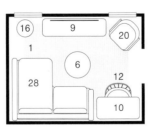

**MEANT FOR LOUNGING**

10' W x 13' D

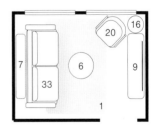

**UNIQUE & THOUGHTFUL**

10' W x 13' D

03.  Organize! The console in this recipe has cabinets that provide plenty of space to stow your remotes, small electronics, and other TV accoutrements. The side table has two open shelves. Floating shelves provide space to display personal treasures, and the desk features a drawer for office supplies.

04.  Light it up. In this living room, I layered the lighting using three different types of fixtures. The overhead semi-flush mount light provides overall illumination. On one side of the couch I set a standing lamp, and on the other side I chose a table lamp with a narrow base to do double duty, providing light for both the couch and the desk.

05.  Watch your step. The large rectangular rug covers nearly the entire floor. I chose a softer, medium-pile rug so you can cozy up on the floor with pillows and throw blankets to watch TV with friends and family. Because this isn't a high-traffic area, you don't have to worry so much about durability.

06.  Accessorize. I like to keep the accessories to a minimum and place just a few decorative but useful bowls and trays on the coffee table and console top. I hung a large mirror on one side of the couch to reflect light and make the room feel larger. Then I installed floating shelves on the other side to give you room to display smaller pieces. I stacked two pieces of framed art above the desk and then finished things off with two potted plants flanking the console and a little baby plant with a trailing vine on the side table. I then added some pillows and a throw blanket for texture and color.

Asymmetrical balance

Tall plants add height

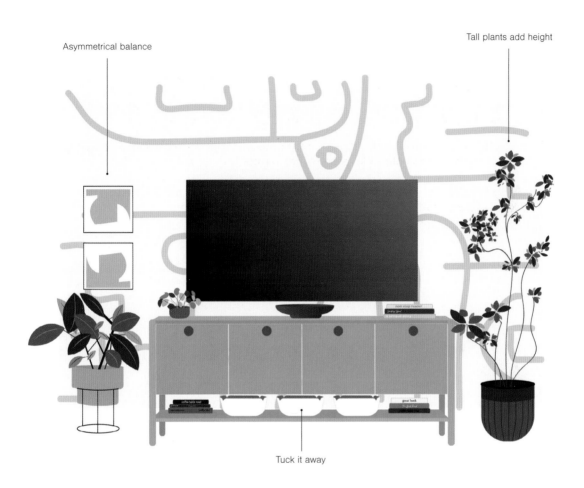

Tuck it away

# Medium Living Room

A medium-sized living room means you'll have room for more seating options—be it an L-shaped sectional or your standard couch and accent chairs setup. The chairs don't have to match the couch, or each other. Some of the best combinations are more eclectic, and you can create a cohesive look by choosing pieces that have similar lines. For this recipe, I've included three different options for room configurations. Feel free to pick and choose elements from each to make your living room your own.

## What You Need:

| Social, Yet Private 12' W x 18' D | Meant for Lounging 12' W x 18' D | A Bit of Everything 12' W x 18' D |
|---|---|---|
| (1) Sofa: 120" W | (1) Sectional: 120" W x 108" D | (1) Sofa: 120" W |
| (1) Coffee Table: 60" x 36" | (1) Coffee Table: 42" Diameter | (2) Large Ottomans |
| (2–3) Side Tables: 20" x 20" | (1) Side Table: 20" x 20" | (2) Side Tables: 20" x 20" |
| (1–2) Accent Chair(s) | (1) Accent Chair | (2) Accent Chairs |
| (1) Credenza: 72" W x 20" D | (1) Credenza: 72" W x 20" D | (1) Credenza: 84" W x 20" D |
| (2) Bookshelves or Cabinets | (1) Semi-Flush Mount | (1) Semi-Flush Mount |
| (1) Semi-Flush Mount | (1) Console: 72–80" L x 12" D | (2) Small Ottomans |
| (1) Area Rug: 9' X 12' | (1) Area Rug: 9' x 12' | (1) Area Rug: 9' X 12' |
| (1) TV: 65–70" | (1) TV: 65–70" | (1) TV: 65–70" |

## Add-Ons:

| | | |
|---|---|---|
| (2–4) Wall Sconces | (1) Table Lamp | (1) Floor Lamp |
| (3) 24" W x 36" H Frames | (1) Runner: 8' x 2'6 | |

01. Assess your space. Refer to your floor plan or sketch things out if that's helpful. Your sketch doesn't have to be perfect, and it will help you envision which elements will work for your particular space.

02. Choose your core components. In the "Social Yet Private" living room shown opposite, I paired a classic long couch with a rectangular coffee table.

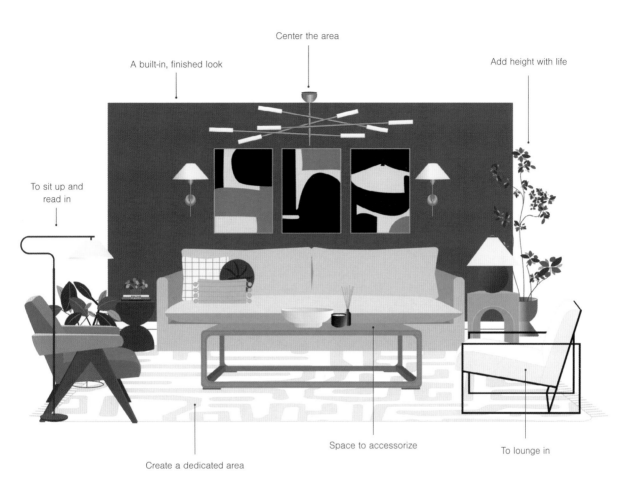

A built-in, finished look

Center the area

Add height with life

To sit up and read in

To lounge in

Space to accessorize

Create a dedicated area

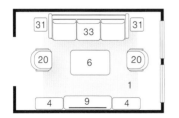

**SOCIAL YET PRIVATE**

12' W x 18' D

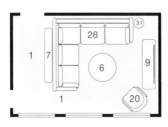

**MEANT FOR LOUNGING**

12' W x 18' D

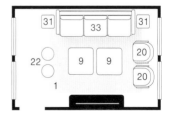

**A BIT OF EVERYTHING**

12' W x 18' D

03. Organize! In this room, two tall cabinets with glass doors flank the TV and console. The shelving provides plenty of space to keep books and display treasures. You could designate one of the cabinets as your bar and store your glassware and bottles inside. The console has cabinets that provide plenty of space to stow your remotes, small electronics, and other TV accoutrements.

04. Light it up. In this living room, I layered the lighting using multiple types of fixtures. The overhead semi-flush mount light provides overall illumination. On one side of the couch I set a table lamp, and next to one of the chairs I placed a standing lamp that's easily adjustable for reading. A sconce light over one side of the couch provides another layer of light and works well with a low-wattage bulb to set a warm, romantic mood. The sconces on each side of the TV are mounted flush to the wall and create an almost cinematic look.

05. Watch your step. The large rectangular rug covers nearly the entire floor. I chose a softer, medium-pile rug so you can cozy up with pillows and throw blankets to watch TV with friends and family. Because this isn't a high-traffic area, you don't have to worry so much about durability.

06. Accessorize. In this room I had more space to play around with, so I chose larger potted plants and created a pleasing vignette on the coffee table with a ceramic bowl, a squat candle, and a little vase. I hung three large, framed pieces above the couch to make a strong visual statement and balance out the height of the TV and cabinets on the opposite wall. I then added a few pillows to the couch for texture and color.

Feature your
personality

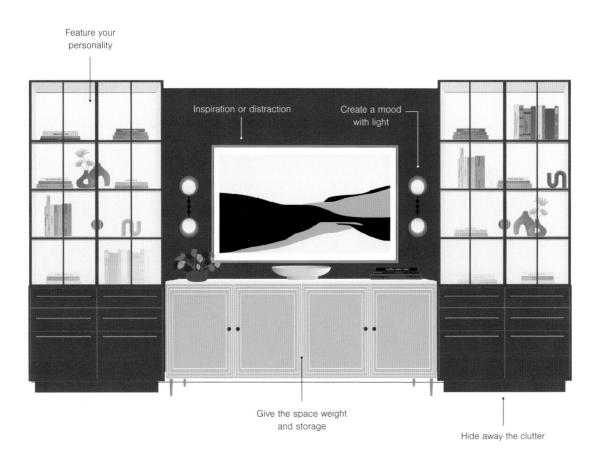

Inspiration or distraction

Create a mood
with light

Give the space weight
and storage

Hide away the clutter

# Open-Concept Living Room

More and more we're living in homes that have open living and dining spaces. These multi-purpose rooms can be a bit of a challenge to configure. This is where zoning comes in handy for designating dedicated activity spaces. For this recipe, I've shown three different options for organizing and furnishing an open-concept room. Feel free to pick and choose elements from each to fit your particular space.

## What You Need:

| Space to Chill 16' W x 20' D | Open & Organized 16' W x 20' D | Cohesive 16' W x 20' D |
|---|---|---|
| (1) Sectional: 132" L x 132" D | (1) Sofa: 120" W | (1) Sofa: 120" W |
| (1) Coffee Table: 60" x 60" | (1) Coffee Table: 60" x 60" | (1) Coffee Table: 60" x 36" |
| (2) Accent Chairs | (2) Side Tables: 20" x 20" | (2) Accent Chairs |
| (2) Side Tables: 20" x 20" | (2) Accent Chairs | (1) Sofa Console |
| (1) Credenza: 84" W x 20" D | (1) Credenza: 84" W x 20" D | (3) Ottomans: 18" Diameter |
| (1) Semi-Flush Mount | (1) Semi-Flush Mount | (1) Credenza: 84" W x 20" D |
| (1) Area Rug: 9' x 12' | (2) Bookcases or Cabinets | (1) Semi-Flush Mount |
| (1) TV: 70–80" | (1) Area Rug: 9' x 12' | (1) Area Rug: 9' x 12' |
| | (1) TV: 70–80" | (1) TV: 70–80" |

## Add-Ons:

| | | |
|---|---|---|
| (2) Bookshelves or Cabinets | (2) Wall Sconces | (1) Table Lamp |
| (1) Floor Lamp | | |

01.  Assess your space. Refer to your floor plan or sketch things out if that's helpful. Your sketch doesn't have to be perfect, and it will help you envision which elements will work for your particular space. Zoning is essential in this recipe so refer back to page 62 for a refresher on how to create specific zones in a room.

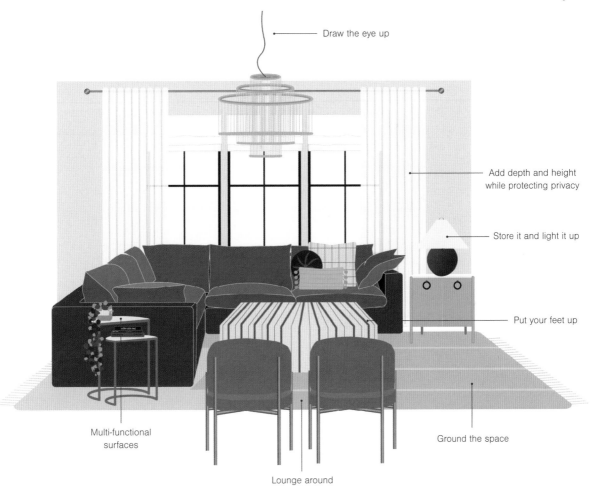

Draw the eye up

Add depth and height while protecting privacy

Store it and light it up

Put your feet up

Multi-functional surfaces

Lounge around

Ground the space

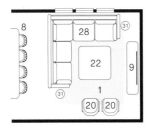

**SPACE TO CHILL**

16' W x 20' D

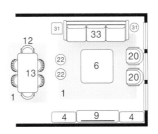

**OPEN AND ORGANIZED**

16' W x 20' D

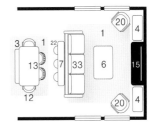

**COHESIVE**

16' W x 20' D

02. Choose your core components. Refer to page 125 for tips on choosing the perfect sofa and coffee table combo. In the "Space to Chill" living room shown opposite, I paired a cushy sectional couch with a sturdy square coffee table that you can rest your feet on or gather around to play a board game. I chose a pair of lightweight upholstered chairs that are easy to move around, and nesting side tables that can be separated so everyone has a spot to put their drinks. Behind the couch, I placed four stools that you can scoot under the countertop when not in use.

03. Organize! Placing a credenza beneath the TV provides ample room to stow your remotes, small electronics, and other TV accoutrements, along with spare throw blankets and pillows. The side table has shelves behind the doors for books, small craft projects, or newspapers and magazines.

04. Light it up. I hung a dramatic chandelier over the couch and set a table lamp with a squat ceramic base on the side table. On each side of the TV, I mounted sconces with dimmers that set the mood. The curtain panels can easily be pulled across to minimize glare on the TV screen. Hanging the curtains 2–4 inches above the top of the windows will create the illusion of higher ceilings.

05. Watch your step. Did you notice how I placed the rug beneath the couch, chairs, and coffee table, but left the floor clear behind the couch? This is to create a traffic lane and differentiate the eating area from the lounging area. I chose a softer, medium-pile rug so you can cozy up on the floor with pillows and throw blankets to watch TV with friends and family. Because this isn't a high-traffic area, you don't have to worry so much about durability.

06. Accessorize. The tall potted plant balances out the height of the TV and I added another smaller plant on the other side. Because the credenza provides plenty of storage, I had room to display a few books and create a little vignette with a shallow bowl, a vase, and a candle. And let's not overlook the adorable little plant baby on the other side of the credenza. A few throw pillows on the couch add texture and color.

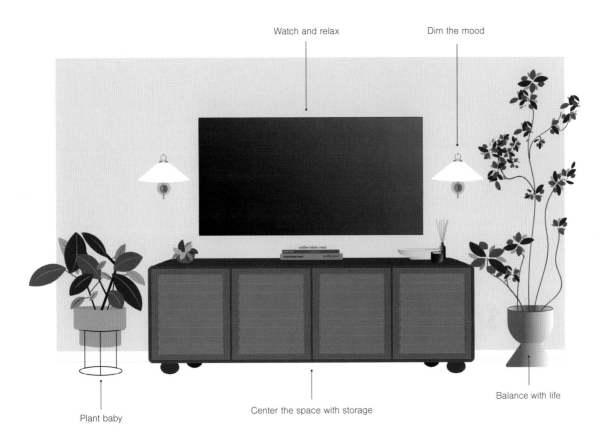

Watch and relax

Dim the mood

Plant baby

Center the space with storage

Balance with life

# Long, Narrow Living Room

Oh, the awkward long living room! In this sort of long, narrow space, it can be hard to figure out where things should go. On the plus side though, because you have more space to work with, the room can serve multiple purposes. You could create a reading nook or a conversation pit of sorts with an extra seating area. Think about how you like to spend your time and design the space to accommodate your unique needs. In this recipe, I've included four different configurations for four different room sizes. Don't limit yourself—take inspiration from any of these examples and apply it to your own particular space.

## What You Need:

| Tucked Away<br>10' W x 9' D | Daily Function<br>12' W x 20' D |
|---|---|
| (1) Sofa: 84" W | (1) Sofa: 96" W |
| (1) Coffee Table: 56" W x 24" D | (1) Coffee Table: 56" W x 24" D |
| (2) Side Tables 18" x 18" | (2) Side Tables: 20" x 20" |
| (2) Ottomans 18" Diameter | (1) Credenza: 72" W x 20" D |
| (2) Bookshelves or Cabinets: 42" W | (1) Semi-Flush Mount, Chandelier, or Fan |
| (1) Accent Chair | (2) Accent Chairs |
| (1) Credenza: 72" W x 20" D | (1) Low Storage Cabinets: 60"W |
| (1) Semi-Flush Mount, Chandelier, or Fan | (1) Bookcase or Cabinet: 60" W |
| (1) Area Rug: 8' x 10' | (1) Area Rug: 8' x 10' |
| (1) TV: 55–65" | (1) TV: 55–65" |

## Add-Ons:

| | |
|---|---|
| (2) Wall Sconces | Curtain Rod & Curtains |
| (1) Table Lamp | Roman or Roller Shades |
| (1) Floor Lamp | (2) 20" W x 20" H Frames |
| (1) 16" W x 20" H Frame | (1) 12" W x 15" H Frame |

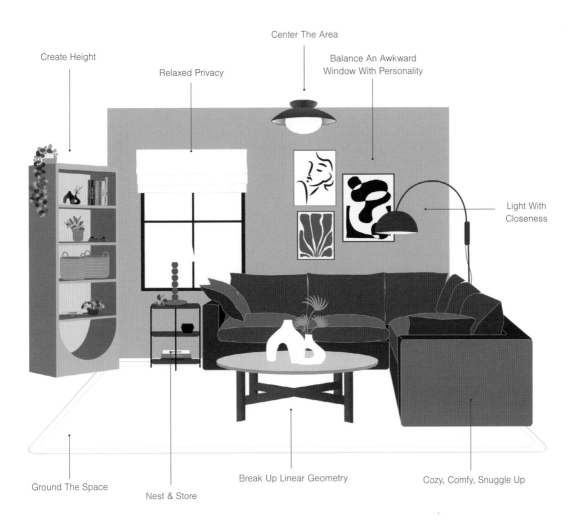

Create Height

Relaxed Privacy

Center The Area

Balance An Awkward Window With Personality

Light With Closeness

Ground The Space

Nest & Store

Break Up Linear Geometry

Cozy, Comfy, Snuggle Up

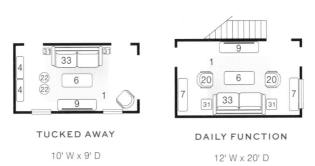

**TUCKED AWAY**

10' W x 9' D

**DAILY FUNCTION**

12' W x 20' D

| | |
|---|---|
| (1) 8" W x 10" H Frame | (1) Mirror: 36" Round |
| (3-5) Pillows | (1-2) Medium Plants |
| (3) Small Plants | (1) Large Tall Plant |
| (1) Catchall Bowl | (2) Ottomans: 18" Diameter |

01. Assess your space. Refer to your floor plan or sketch things out if that's helpful. Your sketch doesn't have to be perfect, and it will help you envision which elements will work for your particular space. Zoning is essential in this recipe, so refer back to page 62 for a refresher on how to create specific zones in a room.

02. Choose your core components. Refer to page 125 for tips on choosing the perfect sofa and coffee table combo. In the A Space to Grow living room shown opposite, I paired a sectional couch with classic lines with a round coffee table. The round shape of the table balances out the sharp angles of the couch. You might notice that, throughout this room, I used round shapes as a counterpoint to the long rectangular shape of the room. I then created a secondary lounge zone with two chairs and a small round coffee table. Behind the chairs, I placed a low open shelving unit that spans the staircase wall. Its clean lines and short depth make it unobtrusive, yet it remains fully functional.

03. Organize! I placed a tall bookcase next to the TV for storage. This room has a fireplace beneath the TV, but if you don't have a fireplace, I recommend placing a credenza with cabinets here to stash your remotes, small electronics, and other TV accoutrements, along with spare throw blankets and pillows.

04. Light it up. A semi-flush mount light casts ambient light over the lounge area while a table lamp on the low bookshelf illuminates that secondary lounge zone. The standing lamp behind the couch directs light for reading, and a table lamp on the side table provides additional light at a lower level. Two wall sconces on the staircase wall highlight the artwork. When lowered, the Roman shades block out light and reduce glare on the TV screen.

05. Watch your step. The rugs designate the two different zones and leave plenty of room for traffic. I chose a round rug with a low pile for the secondary lounge area and a square rug with higher pile for the primary lounge area. Because the pathways through the room are clear, you don't need to worry about selecting a rug made from more durable fibers. In this case, I went with a wool shag rug.

06. Accessorize. I stacked two framed pieces of art on the staircase wall to balance out the height of the stairwell itself. I also hung two smaller pieces above the low bookshelf. Staggering the height of the two pieces is an elegant solution for filling the awkward space. Arrange books, ceramics, or other accessories on the bookshelves and you'll have a beautifully appointed living room with lots of personality. Note: If you don't have a bookshelf, you can always opt for a tall houseplant in that space.

Highlight You

Create interest

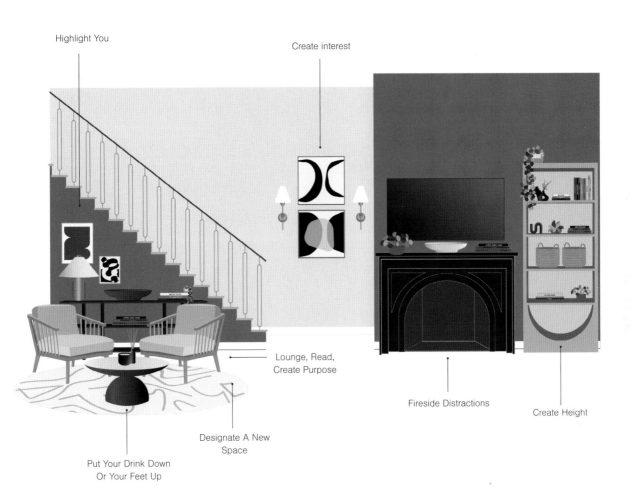

Lounge, Read,
Create Purpose

Fireside Distractions

Create Height

Designate A New
Space

Put Your Drink Down
Or Your Feet Up

# Media Walls

A media wall doesn't have to be strictly utilitarian. You can customize the wall with art-work, floating shelves, wall sconces, bookshelves, and plants. On this page you'll find six different ways to configure your media center, but don't feel limited by these options. Use them for inspiration and mix and match to tailor the wall to your taste.

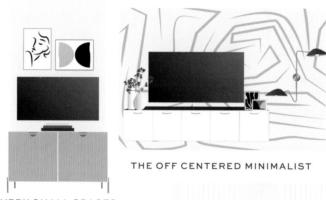

THE OFF CENTERED MINIMALIST

VERY SMALL SPACES

124

FUNCTIONAL MADNESS

THE WINDOW WALL

A BLENDED APPROACH

THE ILLUSION OF HEIGHT

# Sofa & Coffee Table Combos

Hey! Want to know a design secret? Choose your sofa and coffee table as a combo. That's the best way to achieve balance and function in a living room. Check out the options here to determine what sort of piece will work best with what you already have.

### COHESIVE NEST

TYPE: Open base sofa + nesting tables
MATERIAL: Wood frame sofa + metal or stone tables
COLOR: Light sofa fabric + medium/dark coffee tables

### OPEN & RELAXED

TYPE: Open base sofa + open base oval table
MATERIAL: Wood or metal frame sofa + dark wood table
COLOR: Light sofa fabric + dark coffee table

### COZY CORNER

TYPE: To-the-floor sectional + drum table or ottoman
MATERIAL: Fabric sofa + wood or stone table
COLOR: Light sofa fabric + medium/dark coffee table

### RELAX A BIT

TYPE: To-the-floor sectional + round off the ground coffee table
MATERIAL: Fabric sofa + wood, stone, and metal table
COLOR: Medium/dark sofa fabric + light coffee table

125

### STRETCH OUT

TYPE: Open base sofa + open base rectangular table
MATERIAL: Fabric sofa with wood or metal legs + wood table
COLOR: Medium/dark sofa fabric + dark coffee table

### HIDE AWAY

TYPE: To-the-floor sofa + open base storage table
MATERIAL: Fabric sofa + wood table
COLOR: Light/medium sofa fabric + medium wood coffee table

### ORGANIZED & CLEAN

TYPE: Open base sofa + open base storage table
MATERIAL: Leather sofa with wood legs + wood table
COLOR: Medium leather + dark wood coffee table

### INTIMATE WAYS

TYPE: To-the-floor sofa + two ottomans
MATERIAL: Fabric sofa + fabric ottomans
COLOR: Medium/dark sofa fabric + light fabric ottomans

# CHAPTER SEVEN

# Dining Room

The dining room is where we gather around the table—not just to eat and entertain, but also to work, play games, craft, or simply relax with a cup of tea. It doesn't matter whether you have a palatial dining room with a table for twelve or a small dining nook in the kitchen; these recipes will show you how to make the most of your space. I'll walk you through the key pieces, show you plenty of clever storage solutions, and give you some tips on how to mix and match for maximum effect.

# Dining Nook

Sometimes all you need (or all you get!) is a little corner. This recipe shows how to make the most of a limited space or how to create a secondary dining area in your kitchen or living area. Don't limit yourself—take inspiration from these examples and apply it to your own particular space.

## What You Need:

| The Focused Minimalist<br>7' W x 7' D | The Intimate Experience<br>8' W x 8' D | Functional Family Style<br>8' W x 9' D |
|---|---|---|
| (1) Dining Table: 36" W | (1) Dining Table: 42" W | Dining Table: 60" W |
| (1–2) Bench(es) | (1) Area Rug: 6' Round | (2) Benches |
| (2) Dining Chairs | (2) Linear Sconces | (2) Dining Chairs |
| | (2) Benches | |
| | (2) Dining Chairs | |

## Add-Ons:

| | | |
|---|---|---|
| (1) Chandelier | Roman or Roller Shades | (2–3) Candle Holders |
| (1) Droopy Plant | (1) Large Vase | |

01.  Assess your space. Refer to your floor plan or sketch things out if that's helpful. Your sketch doesn't have to be perfect, and it will help you envision which elements will work for your particular space.

02.  Choose your core components. Pedestal tables work well in dining nooks. They're easier to maneuver around and the open space beneath them makes it less likely that you'll bump knees with others at the table. I recommend open-back chairs to create the feel of openness and space.

For this recipe, I chose a small pedestal table and set a pair of chairs on one side and a bench on the other. The bench can be either a standalone or built-in. Make sure you leave enough room for folks to slide onto the bench from either side of the table.

For corner dining nooks, I like using a built-in L-shaped bench and two casual chairs for seating around the small pedestal table.

Allow the light

Create a mood

Squeeze on in

Create contrast

A place to dine

**THE FOCUSED MINIMALIST**

Seats 2–4 people

7' W x 7' D

**THE INTIMATE EXPERIENCE**

Seats 2–4 People

8' W x 8' D

**FUNCTIONAL FAMILY STYLE**

Seats 4–6 people

8' W x 9' D

03. Organize! Space is at a minimum in these small nooks, so make the most of what you have. You can slide storage baskets beneath the bench—perfect for storing soft items like tablecloths, table runners, and napkins. A banquette will help maximize how much seating you can provide. You can squish lots of bums on a banquette! And bonus: it has plenty of storage beneath the seats—perfect for storing larger items you don't need at readily at hand.

04. Light it up. Make sure to scale your lighting to the size of the space. I hung a fan light over the table and opted not to use window treatments. Instead, I let the ambient light flow through the unobstructed windows. Horizontal wall sconces shed light downward on both the artwork and the table itself.

05. Watch your step. If space allows, a round rug defines the space and echoes the shape of the table-top. It also makes for a nice counterpoint to the sharp angles of the bench.

06. Accessorize. Keep it simple! Because the tabletops are small, you'll want to leave as much room as possible for dining. Two tall candleholders with taper candles add height and take up just a few inches of tabletop space. If the tabletop is big enough, I like placing a medium-sized vase with branches to add height. I placed a single large piece of art above the bench for a dramatic focal point. If you have a backless bench, make sure you leave plenty of room, so no one hits their head! Artwork should be mounted 18–20 inches above the bench seat if there's no back, or 8–10 inches above a bench with a back.

▶ **PRO TIP:** Consider seat height! When you're using a combination of benches, banquettes, and chairs, it can be easy to end up with different seat heights. Try to choose chairs with seats at equal heights so no one feels like the little kid at the table. I recommend keeping a dining chair height of 18 inches high.

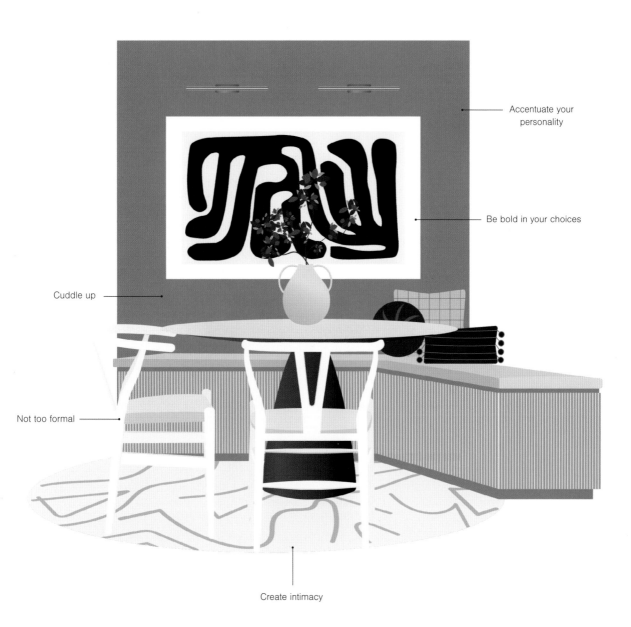

Accentuate your
personality

Be bold in your choices

Cuddle up

Not too formal

Create intimacy

# Small Dining Room

Many apartments feature a small, bistro-style dining area in the corner of the kitchen or great room. These recipes also work well for small patios or for a coffee zone in a larger living room!

## What You Need:

(1) Dining Table: 30–34"          (2–4) Dining Chairs          (1) Area Rug: 6' Round

## Add-Ons:

(6) 20" W x 20" H Frames          (1) Pendant or Chandelier          (2–3) Candle Holders

01.  Assess your space. Refer to your floor plan or sketch things out if that's helpful. Your sketch doesn't have to be perfect and it will help you envision what elements will work for your particular space.

02.  Choose your core components. I like pedestal tables for small dining rooms because they have a single base rather than four legs that can make pushing chairs beneath the table challenging in a small space. For pedestal tables with wider bases, the open lines of the chairs can balance out the wideness of the base.

03.  Light it up. Make sure to scale your lighting to the size of the space.

04.  Accessorize. The small size of these spaces doesn't allow for much surface area other than the tabletop, so I focused on accessorizing the walls. To create height and make a strong statement, I like to stack six square framed pieces of art in pairs. The configuration creates a wallpaper effect of sorts. To give depth to the space, I paint the walls a darker shade and then hang various-sized artwork in two groupings. Using an equal number of pieces on each wall keeps the arrangements from looking haphazard or cluttered.

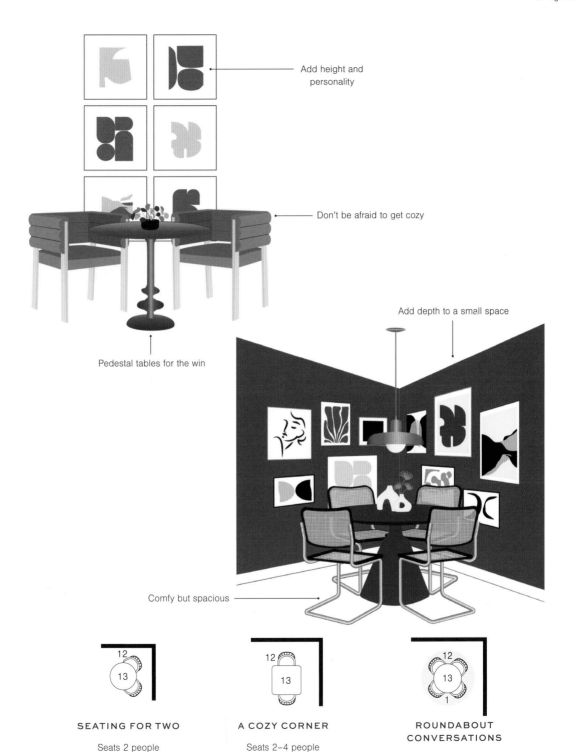

Add height and personality

Don't be afraid to get cozy

Add depth to a small space

Pedestal tables for the win

Comfy but spacious

**SEATING FOR TWO**

Seats 2 people
6' W x 6' D

**A COZY CORNER**

Seats 2–4 people
7' W x 7' D

**ROUNDABOUT CONVERSATIONS**

Seats 2–4 people
8' W x 8' D

# Medium Dining Room

The more space you have, the more elements you can add. But as with every room, be mindful of function. Make sure the pieces you choose work in your particular space. And if possible, choose pieces that have built-in storage. I've included three different recipes for three different room sizes, but don't limit yourself. Feel free to pick and choose elements from each recipe for your own dining room.

## What You Need:

| Cozy Intent<br>10' W x 10' D | Social Cohesion<br>10' W x 11' D | Traditional Setup<br>10' W x 12' D |
|---|---|---|
| (1) Dining Table: 42–48" Round | (1) Dining Table: 60" W | (1) Dining Table: 72" x 36" |
| (4) Dining Chairs | (4) Dining Chairs | (4) Dining Chairs |
| (1) Area Rug: 8' Round | (2) Accent End Dining Chairs | (2) Accent Dining Chairs |
| (1) Console: 72" W x 12–15" D | (1) Area Rug: 6' x 9' | (1) Area Rug: 6' x 9' |
| (1) Chandelier: 30" W | (1) Console: 72" W x 12–15" D | (1) Credenza: 72" x 20" |
| | (1) Chandelier: 36" W | (1) Chandelier: 48" W |

## Add-Ons:

| | | |
|---|---|---|
| (2) Bookcases or Cabinets | (1) Bench: 48" W | |

01. Assess your space. Refer to your floor plan or sketch things out if that's helpful. Your sketch doesn't have to be perfect, and it will help you envision which elements will work for your particular space.

02. Choose your core components. And remember that dining tables don't have to be wood! You could go with a glass top, Formica, or even a marble top. For this dining room I chose a teak table with legs on a diagonal. At the shorter ends of the table, I placed chairs with washable slipcovers. If you go this route, make sure you choose a stain-resistant fabric. On the longer sides of the table, I placed wicker-backed chairs with wooden bases. You could also swap in a bench on one side. Notice how this table setup uses three different tones—the lightest for the slipcovered chairs, the medium tone for the table, and the darker accent color for the chair legs on the wicker-backed chairs.

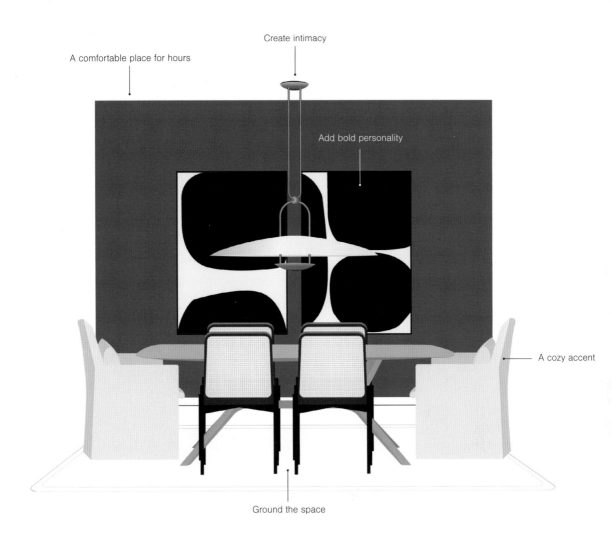

Create intimacy

A comfortable place for hours

Add bold personality

A cozy accent

Ground the space

**COZY INTENT**

Seats 4 people
10' W x 10' D

**SOCIAL COHESION**

Seats 4–6 people
10' W x 11' D

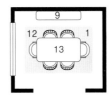

**TRADITIONAL SETUP**

Seats 6 people
10' W x 12' D

03. Organize! The credenza provides roomy cupboards in which to store extra dishware, table linens, and serving pieces. If you don't need storage space, you could opt for an open console to give the room a more open look.

04. Light it up. The wide shade on the hanging fixture does a beautiful job of distributing light across the surface of the tabletop. On the wall above the credenza, I mounted two sconces with shades and positioned a mirror in between to reflect the light and make the space feel larger.

05. Watch your step. I placed a rectangular rug beneath the table and chairs. I recommend choosing a low-pile carpet. Low-pile carpets make it easy to scoot chairs in and out from the table and they're also easy to sweep or vacuum. Make sure your rug extends 24" from the table so your chair doesn't get caught on the edge of the rug.

06. Accessorize. I hung a bold geometric painting on the long wall behind the table. On the opposite wall, I hung a mirror over the credenza and set a potted plant on each side. The taller plant adds height and drama. On top of the credenza, I arranged a wide-mouthed ceramic bowl, a candle, and a little vase.

▸ PRO TIP: Consider a darker, moodier color for your dining room walls. It will add depth and drama and will make candlelight even more romantic.

Accentuate it

Reflect light

Add height

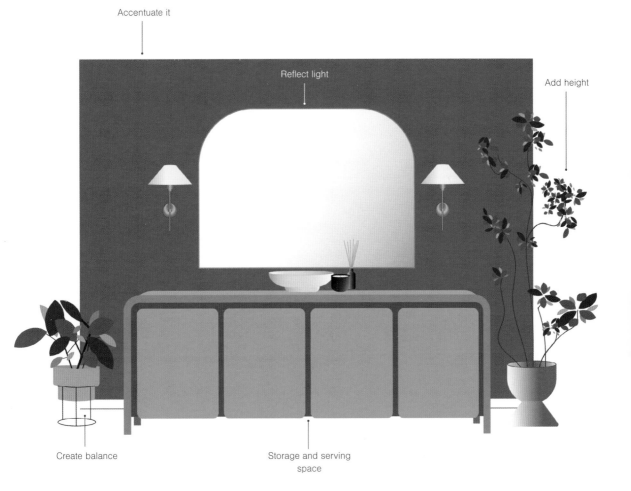

Create balance

Storage and serving space

# Large Dining Room

Hello, sophistication! Oftentimes, homes with large dining rooms also have an additional casual dining space off the kitchen or living area. If that's the case in your house, then you can lean heavily into the style elements in the large dining room and not worry so much about storage. You also have the freedom to not worry so much about durability, which opens up a lot of style possibilities. I've included three different recipes for three different room sizes. Each room includes the same core elements, just at different sizes, so feel free to mix and match.

## What You Need:

| The Comfortable Type 11' W x 14' D | Open & Airy 12' W x 15' D | Made for Entertainment 14' W x 16' D |
|---|---|---|
| (1) Dining Table: 84" W | (1) Dining Table: 96" W x 39" D | (1) Dining Table: 108" W x 42" D |
| (4) Dining Chairs | (6) Dining Chairs | (6) Dining Chairs |
| (2) Accent Dining Chairs | (2) Accent Dining Chairs | (2) Accent Dining Chairs |
| (1) Area Rug: 8' x 10' | (1) Area Rug: 9' x 12' | (1) Area Rug: 9' x 12' |
| (1) Credenza: 72" W | (1) Credenza: 72" W | (1) Credenza: 84" W |
| (1) Chandelier | (1) Chandelier | (1) Chandelier |

## Add-Ons:

| | | |
|---|---|---|
| (1) Table Extension: 100" | | |

01. Assess your space. Refer to your floor plan or sketch things out if that's helpful. Your sketch doesn't have to be perfect, and it will help you envision which elements will work for your particular space.

02. Choose your core components. In a large dining room, the table will be the centerpiece that you build the rest of the room around. For this large dining room, I chose a large rectangular wood table with a darker finish. Because the base is made of solid wood panels, I surrounded the table with chairs with open construction to provide counterbalance.

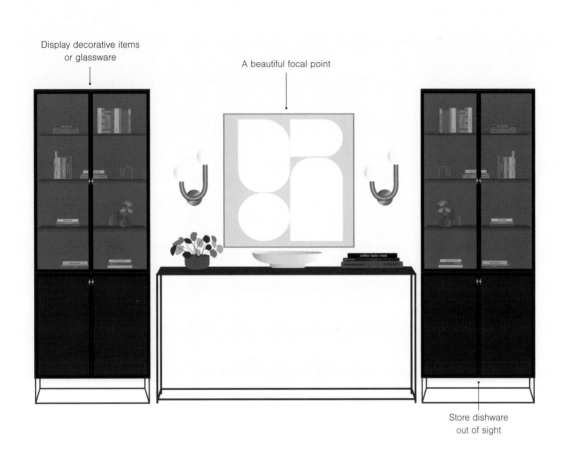

Display decorative items or glassware

A beautiful focal point

Store dishware out of sight

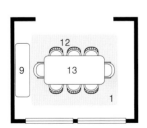

**THE COMFORTABLE TYPE**

Seats 6–8 people

11' W x 14' D

**OPEN & AIRY**

Seats 6–8 people

12' W x 15' D

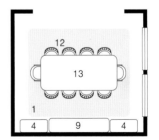

**MADE FOR ENTERTAINMENT**

Seats 10–12 People

14' W x 16' D

03. Organize! Two cabinets flank the console and provide lots of room to store extra dishware out of sight in the cupboards below. The glass doors on the upper cabinets let you display pretty glassware or decorative pieces. Because the cabinets provide ample storage, I used an open console with a slim profile to complement the sturdier table.

04. Light it up. I hung a dramatic chandelier above the table and positioned two sconces on the wall above the console to highlight the artwork. For the window treatment, I opted for simple sheers to let light filter in during the day. I hung the panels about one foot above the top of the window frame. The length of the panels suspended from that height lends an air of sophistication to the room.

05. Watch your step. I placed a large rectangular rug beneath the table and chairs. I recommend choosing a low-pile carpet that's easy to sweep or vacuum. Low-pile carpets also make it easy to scoot chairs in and out from the table. Make sure your rug extends 24" wider than the table so the chair legs won't get caught on the edge.

06. Accessorize. I hung a bold geometric painting on the wall above the credenza for a focal point. The tabletop is roomy enough for a large vase with seasonal branches. Of course, you'll want to move the vase off the table at mealtime so guests can see each other when seated!

Add drama and elegance

Let the light in

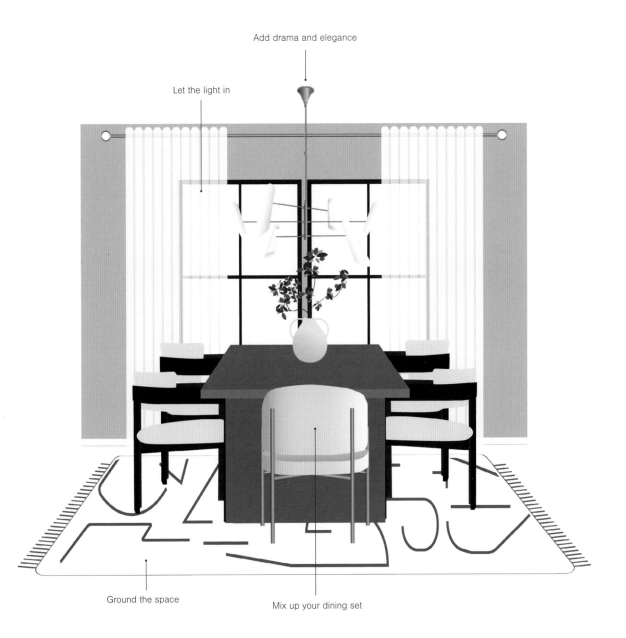

Ground the space

Mix up your dining set

# How to Create Cohesion by Mixing & Matching

How do you create cohesion when mixing and matching? I get asked this question a ton!
If you don't want a full matching dining room set (which I don't recommend!), here are
eight ways you can achieve a curated look.

### SWAP YOUR END CHAIRS

Mix soft upholstery and hard materials to create contrast.

### USE THE RULE OF THREE

Keep one of each: light, medium, and dark tone. Consider
three different colors, textures, or patterns to keep you on
track with mixing and matching.

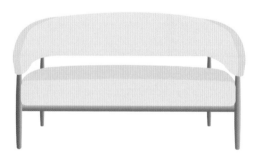

### SWAP YOUR END CHAIRS

Mix soft upholstery and hard materials to create contrast.

### ADD A BENCH

Break it up with a bench or banquette; something you
wouldn't see in everyone's home, just yours.

## MAKE IT ECLECTIC

Mix it up by using the same chair, but in different colors.

## CONSIDER THE DECADE

Mix chairs that were designed in the same decade; things that have a similar stylistic choice.

## MIX MATERIALS

Try mixing materials, like wood and leather, upholstery and metal, or wood and granite.

## PLAY WITH SHAPE

Choose a rounded back chair and a chair with a straight back to create contrast.

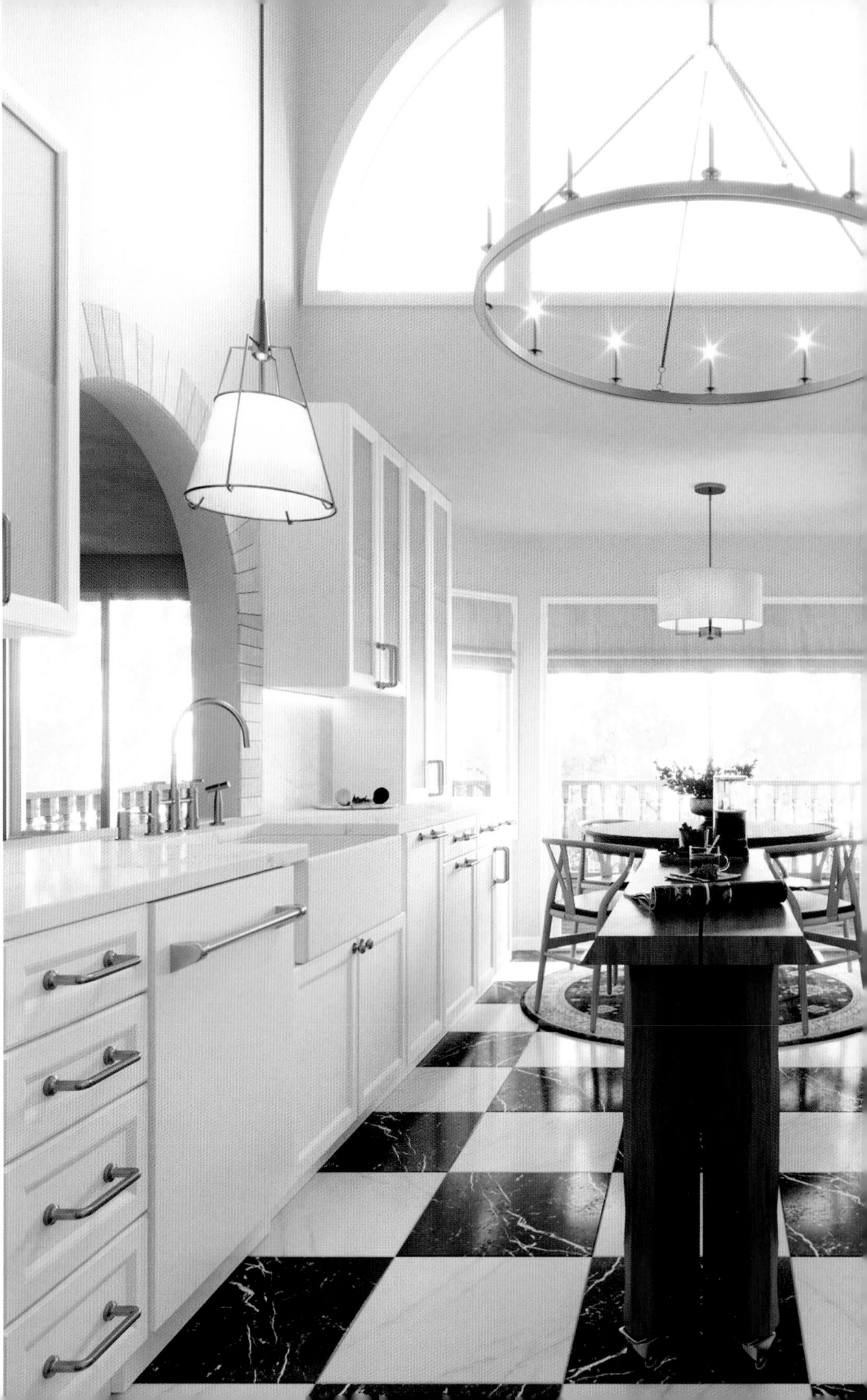

# CHAPTER EIGHT

# Kitchen

Kitchen design doesn't have to be complicated. Whether you're doing a simple refresh or a full-on remodel, you'll be amazed at what you can achieve with some planning and creativity. In this chapter, I'll cover tricks and tips to achieving a gorgeous, fully functional kitchen.

No matter the size or shape of your kitchen, the secret to success is implementing the kitchen triangle. Developed by Lillian Moller Gilbreth in the 1920s, the kitchen triangle represents the pathways between your main appliances. Designers across the globe still follow this simple methodology. It's a matter of arranging your stove, refrigerator, and sink in a triangle configuration to eliminate unnecessary steps from one side of the kitchen to the other. Most kitchens are already designed this way. I've marked the floor plans with the triangle itself so you can easily see how it plays out in kitchens of different shapes and sizes.

One last tip before you get started: It's best to think long term when approaching kitchen design. It's not easy (or sustainable) to change out larger appliances. So, before you spring for that double-decker convection oven, take a minute to think about whether you'll really use two ovens. I know I sound like a broken record, but I'll say it again: think about your particular habits and routines and design your space accordingly.

# Line Kitchen

A line kitchen is exactly what it sounds like: everything is lined up against one wall. Most commonly found in open-concept homes, line kitchens pack a lot into minimal space. The biggest challenge is maximizing the countertops. Efficient storage systems are essential—everything must have a place. This recipe offers three different floor plans, as well as diagrams for two that will show you different options for making the most of your space.

## What You Need:

(1) Sink: 30" W

(1) Dishwasher: 24" W

(1) Refrigerator 24-30" W

(1) Range: 30" W

(1) Range Hood or Microwave Hood

(1) Runner: 8' L

## Add-Ons:

(1) Pot Rail

Floating Shelves

(2) Sconces or (1) Pendant

01. Assess your space. Refer to your floor plan or sketch things out if that's helpful.

02. Organize! Remove everything from your cabinets and write up an inventory list. Yes, I'm serious, list it all out. Next, assign items to each cabinet. Keep items you use regularly in easy-to-reach cupboards and drawers. With closed upper and lower cabinets, you can store everything away for an ultra-clean look. Use the open shelving for your dishware and other items you need readily at hand. Because everything is out in the open on the shelves, I try to arrange items in a pleasing way. You can then store more bulky kitchen gadgets in the cabinets below.

03. Light it up. Most line kitchens rely on a combination of overhead lighting and task lighting. I positioned puck lights below the upper cupboards for focused task lighting. I hung task lighting over the open shelves to cast light downward onto the countertops.

04. Watch your step. It's likely your line kitchen is a pass-through space in your home. For both of these layouts, I chose a runner to ground the space and to catch debris. Be sure to choose a durable fiber with nonslip backing—ideally washable.

05. Accessorize. For both of these line kitchens, I kept decor to a minimum. Given that countertop space is at a premium, you'll want to keep every spare inch free. I recommend just a small decorative plant or vase tucked in a corner.

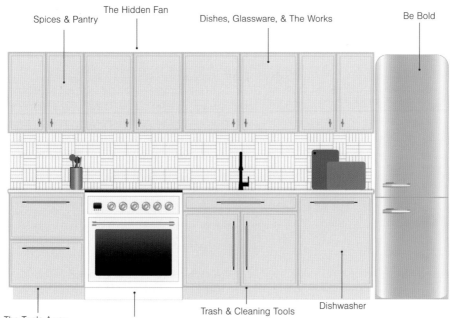

Spices & Pantry
The Hidden Fan
Dishes, Glassware, & The Works
Be Bold

Hide The Tools Away
Something Good Is Cooking
Trash & Cleaning Tools
Dishwasher

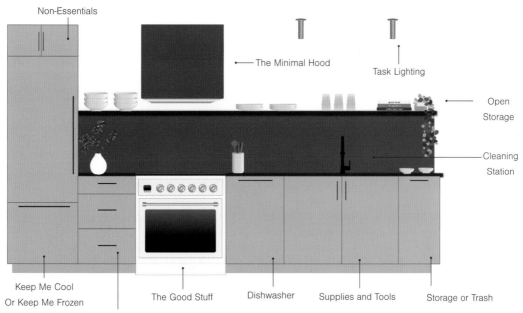

Non-Essentials
The Minimal Hood
Task Lighting
Open Storage
Cleaning Station

Keep Me Cool Or Keep Me Frozen
The Good Stuff
Dishwasher
Supplies and Tools
Storage or Trash

Tools, Pantry, & Spices

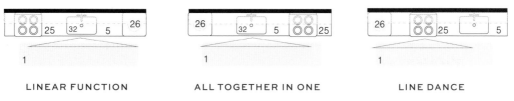

**LINEAR FUNCTION**
12' W x 6' D

**ALL TOGETHER IN ONE**
12' W x 6' D

**LINE DANCE**
12' W x 6' D

# Galley Kitchen

This is the most common kitchen type. The layout is super functional and straightforward—but galley kitchens can easily become overcrowded. This recipe includes lots of tips and tricks showing how to establish efficient storage systems. I've included three different floor plans and a diagram for a standard configuration.

## What You Need:

| | |
|---|---|
| (1) Sink: 30" W | (1) Dishwasher: 24" W |
| (1) Range: 30" W | (1) Range Hood or Microwave Hood |
| (1) Refrigerator 30–36" W | (1) Runner: 8–12' L |

## Add-Ons:

| | |
|---|---|
| (1) Pot Rail | (2) Sconces or (1) Pendant |
| (1) Pot Filler | Roman or Roller Shade |
| (1) Bench | (1) Round Dining Table: 36" |
| (2) Dining Chairs | |

01. Assess your space. Refer to your floor plan or sketch things out if that's helpful. Your sketch doesn't have to be perfect, and it will help you envision which elements will work for your particular space.

02. Organize! Remove everything from your cabinets and write up an inventory list. Yes, I'm serious, list it all out. Next, assign items to each cabinet. Keep items you use regularly in easy-to-reach cupboards and drawers. The closed upper and lower cabinets provide ample space to store everything away. The tall cabinet opposite the refrigerator works well as a pantry and the narrow upper cabinets flanking the microwave offer handy storage for spices and oils. I installed open shelving on one side of the kitchen for cookbooks and decorative items.

▶ PRO TIP: What's your favorite dish to cook? Or your favorite go-to weeknight meal? Take out all the ingredients, utensils, and small appliances you need for your top two to three meals. Then put them away in places that are easy to access. Use this as a model to organize the rest of your kitchen items—it's all about what you use most and need easy access to.

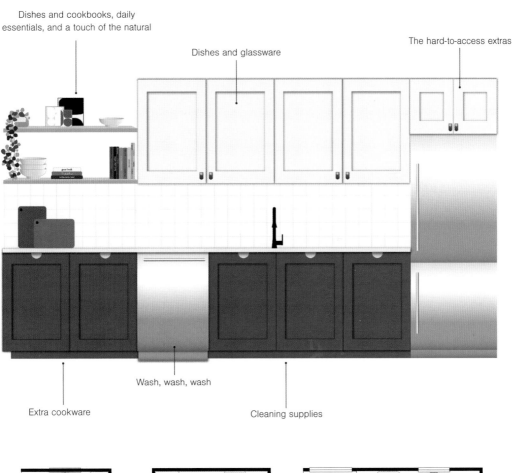

Dishes and cookbooks, daily essentials, and a touch of the natural

Dishes and glassware

The hard-to-access extras

Wash, wash, wash

Extra cookware

Cleaning supplies

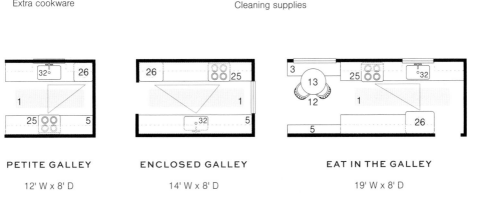

**PETITE GALLEY**

12' W x 8' D

**ENCLOSED GALLEY**

14' W x 8' D

**EAT IN THE GALLEY**

19' W x 8' D

03. Light it up. Consider your natural light levels. Bright task lighting is essential in a kitchen, especially for chopping, but natural light is just as important! If you have a window in your kitchen, I recommend installing a Roman shade that you can keep open most of the time. In this kitchen, I positioned puck lights below the upper cupboards for focused task lighting and then relied on recessed overhead lights for ambient light.

04. Watch your step. A long runner grounds the space and catches debris. Be sure to choose a durable fiber with nonslip backing—ideally washable.

05. Accessorize. The open shelves provide a spot for decorative items and cookbooks. I set a little potted plant with a trailing vine on one side and a pretty dish on the other. I put the cookbooks on the lower shelf for easy access. If you have a window in your galley kitchen, you could add a plant rail for potted herbs. How nice to pluck a sprig of mint from your windowsill to garnish your drink!

▶ PRO TIP: No one said the finish on your hardware has to match. Your faucet can have a different finish than your drawer hardware, and even different from your upper cabinet hardware. Play around and have fun with these elements. They're low commitment, so you can easily change them up for a style refresh.

Dry goods and extra dishes

Spices and oils

Pantry items and small appliances

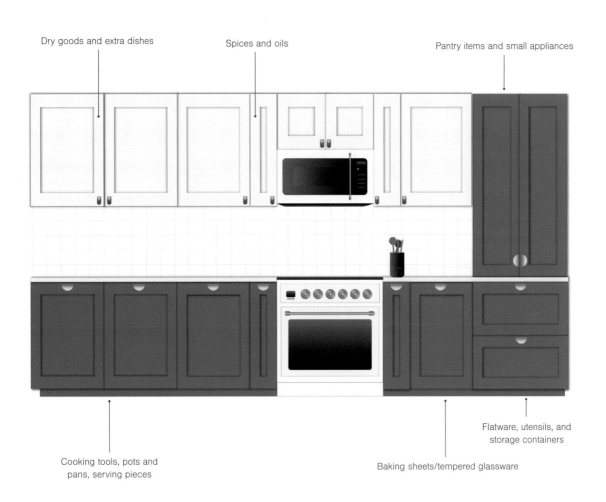

Cooking tools, pots and
pans, serving pieces

Baking sheets/tempered glassware

Flatware, utensils, and
storage containers

# L-Shaped Kitchen

An L-shaped kitchen is tucked into a corner and oftentimes flows right into a dining area. Like galley and line kitchens, counter space is limited, so you'll need to be strategic about where you store your go-to items. This recipe shows three floor plans and a diagram for a standard configuration.

## What You Need:

| | |
|---|---|
| (1) Sink: 30" W | (1) Dishwasher: 24" W |
| (1) Range: 30" W | (1) Range Hood or Microwave Hood |
| (1) Refrigerator: 30–36" W | (1) Runner: 8–12' L |

## Add-Ons:

| | |
|---|---|
| (1) Pot Filler | (2) Sconces Above Sink or (2–3) Pendants |
| Roman or Roller Shade | (2–3) Counter Stools |
| (1) Small Mobile Kitchen Cart | |

01. Assess your space. Refer to your floor plan or sketch things out if that's helpful. Your sketch doesn't have to be perfect, and it will help you envision which elements will work for your particular space.

02. Organize! Remove everything from your cabinets and write up an inventory list. Yes, I'm serious, list it all out. Next, assign items to each cabinet. Keep items you use regularly in easy-to-reach cupboards and drawers. In this kitchen, I added short cabinets above the upper cabinets for extra storage. In the extra bit of space above, I had room for open baskets to store non-essential items.

   ▶ **PRO TIP:** Cook a meal and pay attention to the items you're using and how you're using them. What happens when you take the veggies out of the refrigerator—where do they go? Where does your cutting board sit? When you marinate meat, which part of the counter do you use? This will inform how and where to store things in your kitchen.

03. Light it up. Consider your natural light levels. Bright task lighting is essential in a kitchen, especially for chopping, but natural light is just as important! If you have a window in your kitchen, I recommend installing a Roman shade that you can keep open most of the time. In this kitchen, I positioned puck lights below the upper cupboards for focused task lighting and then relied on recessed overhead lights for the ambient light in the room.

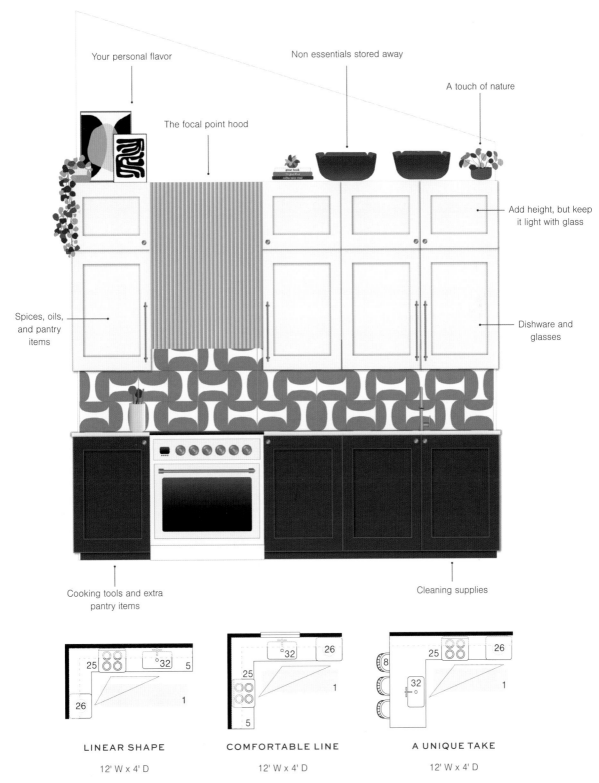

Your personal flavor

Non essentials stored away

A touch of nature

The focal point hood

Add height, but keep it light with glass

Spices, oils, and pantry items

Dishware and glasses

Cooking tools and extra pantry items

Cleaning supplies

**LINEAR SHAPE**

12' W x 4' D

**COMFORTABLE LINE**

12' W x 4' D

**A UNIQUE TAKE**

12' W x 4' D

04. Watch your step. A long runner grounds the space and catches debris. Be sure to choose a durable fiber with nonslip backing—ideally washable.

05. Accessorize. To keep the countertops clear, I used the tops of the upper cabinets to display some framed artwork and two little plants with trailing vines. I then relied on the bold tile on the backsplash and the bronze hood to add personality and color to the room.

▶ **PRO TIP:** Don't worry if you have a tendency to leave dishes for later. I'm guilty of the same. Here's a hack: choose a deeper sink so you can get the dishes off the counter and stack them out of sight in the sink!

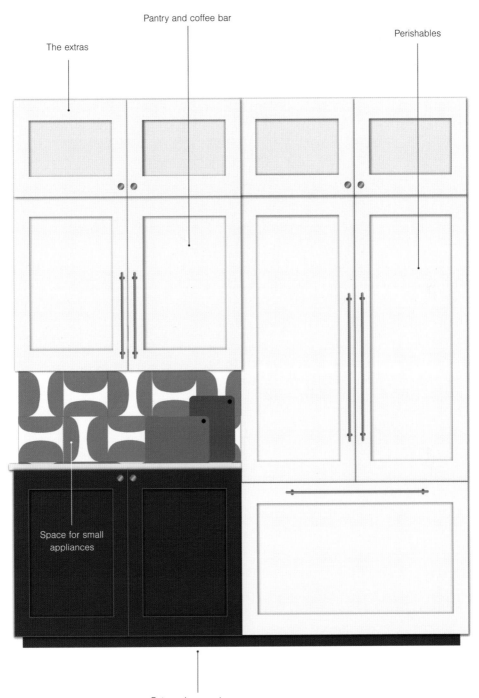

The extras

Pantry and coffee bar

Perishables

Space for small appliances

Pots and pans, storage containers, and serving pieces

# U-Shaped Kitchen

I love U-shaped kitchens. They have so many efficiencies and they're a dream for kitchen triangles! (See page 145 for more info on the kitchen triangle.) This recipe shows three different floor plans, as well as a diagram for a standard configuration.

## What You Need:

(1) Sink: 30" W

(1) Dishwasher: 24" W

(1) Range: 30–36" W

(1) Range Hood or Microwave Hood

(1) Refrigerator: 30–36" W

(1) Runner: 8–12' L

## Add-Ons:

(1) Pot Rail

(1) Pot Filler

(2) Sconces or (1) Pendant

Roman or Roller Shade

(2–3) Counter Stools

01. Assess your space. Refer to your floor plan or sketch things out if that's helpful. Your sketch doesn't have to be perfect, and it will help you envision which elements will work for your particular space.

02. Organize! Remove everything from your cabinets and write up an inventory list. Yes, I'm serious, list it all out. Next, assign items to each cabinet. Keep items you use regularly in easy-to-reach cupboards and drawers. This kitchen features open storage above the countertops on each side of the stove for easy access to dishware, salt and pepper, and other items you need at hand while you cook. The closed storage below provides plenty of space to keep your more utilitarian items off the countertops and out of sight. The pot and pan rail works wonders for keeping your cookware organized and easy to access.

   ▶ PRO TIP: If you're planning your dream kitchen, dream big. Could you add a pot filler above the range? Power outlets inside of kitchen drawers? Or invest in an appliance garage to park your pieces out of sight?

03. Light it up. I positioned a flush mount light on the ceiling above the sink. Then I added sconces above the open shelving to draw the eye upward. For the windows, Roman shades look clean and crisp whether pulled up or down.

Kitchen

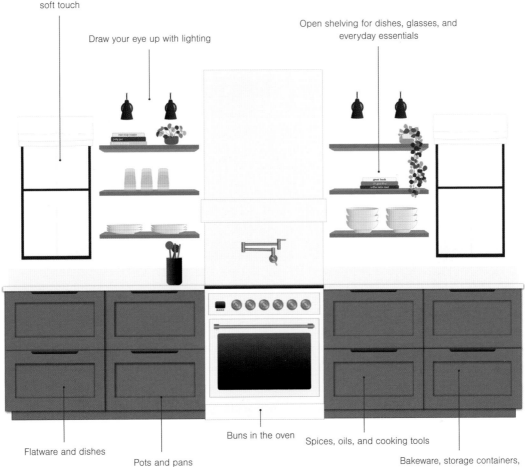

Window treatments for a soft touch

Draw your eye up with lighting

Open shelving for dishes, glasses, and everyday essentials

Flatware and dishes

Pots and pans

Buns in the oven

Spices, oils, and cooking tools

Bakeware, storage containers, and plates

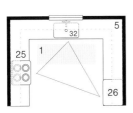

**THE COMFORTABLE TYPE**

Seats 6–8 people

11' W x 14' D

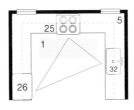

**OPEN & AIRY**

Seats 6–8 people

12' W x 15' D

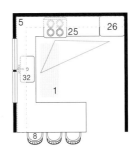

**MADE FOR ENTERTAINMENT**

Seats 10–12 people

10' W x 12' D

04. Watch your step. A rectangular throw rug in front of the sink grounds the space and catches debris. Be sure to choose a durable fiber with nonslip backing—ideally washable.

05. Accessorize. The open shelving works well for cookbooks along with pretty dishware. Over the counters by the sink, I stacked two framed pieces of artwork. On the other side, I hung a pot and pan rail, which not only provides handy storage but also adds visual interest.

   ▶ **PRO TIP**: Consider opting for a shorter backsplash made from the same materials as your countertop! These are typically 4 inches tall, but for a more luxurious look, go 6–12 inches high!

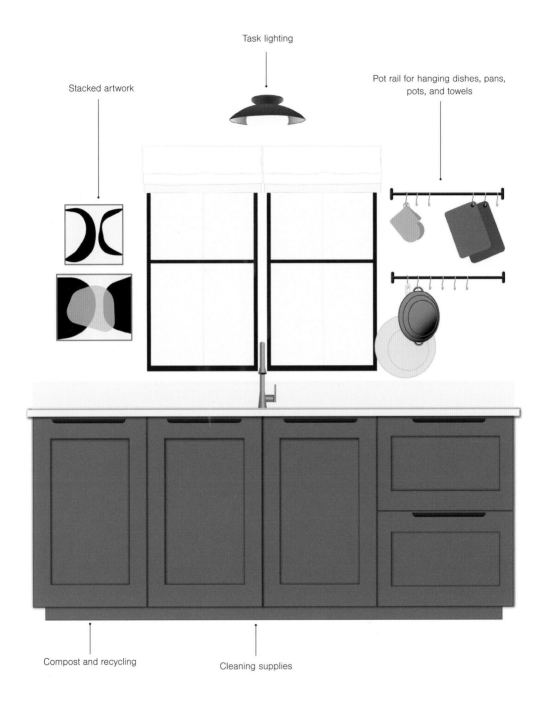

Task lighting

Stacked artwork

Pot rail for hanging dishes, pans, pots, and towels

Compost and recycling

Cleaning supplies

# G-Shaped Kitchen

G-shaped kitchens became popular in the '70s when people moved from less formal meals in their dining rooms to more casual family meals at the counter. I love the cozy and welcoming feel of a G-shaped kitchen. The countertop provides not just a place to dine, but also a great spot for kids to do their homework or guests to sip their drinks while you cook. This recipe shows three different floor plans, as well as a diagram for a standard configuration.

## What You Need:

| | |
|---|---|
| (1) Sink: 30" W | (1) Dishwasher: 24" W |
| (1) Range: 30–36" W | (1) Refrigerator: 30–36" W |
| (1) Runner: 8–12' L | |

## Add-Ons:

| | |
|---|---|
| (1) Pot Filler | (2) Sconces or (2–3) Pendants |
| Roman or Roller Shade | (2–3) Counter Stools |

01. Assess your space. Refer to your floor plan or sketch things out if that's helpful. Your sketch doesn't have to be perfect, and it will help you envision which elements will work for your particular space.

02. Organize! Remove everything from your cabinets and write up an inventory list. Yes, I'm serious, list it all out. Next, assign items to each cabinet. Keep items you use regularly in easy-to-reach cupboards and drawers. This kitchen makes the most of the space beneath the countertops and bar with closed cabinets.

03. Light it up. I mounted sconce lights over the sink. You might consider hanging pendant lights over the bar to provide bright task lighting for kitchen prep work or homework. I left the windows behind the sink unadorned to let in as much natural light as possible.

04. Watch your step. A rectangular throw rug in front of the sink grounds the space and catches debris. Be sure to choose a durable fiber with nonslip backing—ideally washable.

05. Accessorize. Because a G-shaped kitchen can feel closed off, I kept decor to a minimum and made the tiled wall behind the sink the focal point. The full wall of tile draws the eye upward and makes the room feel expansive and airy.

Take tile to the ceiling for a higher-end, dramatic look

Add depth with detailed lighting

Dishes, serveware, and pots and pans

Trash and cleaning supplies

A hidden dishwasher

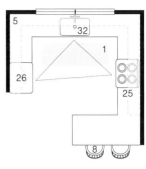

### THE COMFORTABLE TYPE

Seats 6–8 people
11' W x 14' D

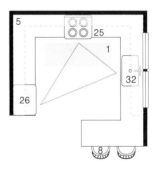

### OPEN & AIRY

Seats 6–8 people
12' W x 15' D

18" overhang for stools

Stools with backs for additional comfort

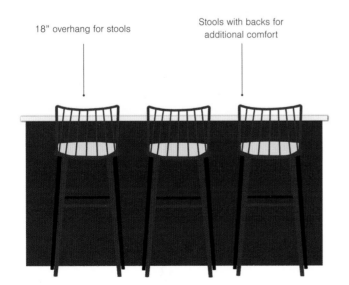

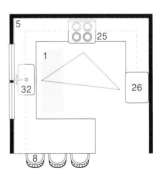

### MADE FOR ENTERTAINMENT

Seats 10–12 people
14' W x 16' D

# Open Concept / Island Kitchen

Open concept kitchens are a more modern take on a galley or line kitchen. They're perfect for entertaining and everyday life! Keep in mind that open concept kitchens literally mean . . . they're open! So, you'll need to think carefully about what you'll store where. I've outlined lots of storage tips and tricks for you to apply to your space. This recipe shows three different floor plans, as well as a diagram for a standard configuration.

## What You Need:

| | |
|---|---|
| (1) Sink: 30–36" W | (1) Dishwasher: 24" W |
| (1) Range: 30–36" W | (1) Range Hood or Microwave Hood |
| (1) Refrigerator: 30–36" W | (1) Runner: 8-12' L |

## Add-Ons:

| | |
|---|---|
| (1) Pot Filler | (2) Sconces or (2–3) Pendants |
| Roman or Roller Shade | (4–6) Counter Stools |

01. Assess your space. Refer to your floor plan or sketch things out if that's helpful. Your sketch doesn't have to be perfect, and it will help you envision which elements will work for your particular space.

02. Organize! Remove everything from your cabinets and write up an inventory list. Yes, I'm serious, list it all out. Next, assign items to each cabinet. Keep items you use regularly in easy-to-reach cupboards and drawers.

   ▶ PRO TIP: If you have the opportunity, look into panel-ready appliances. They'll hide your appliances behind cabinet doors to create a seamless look that will make your kitchen feel sleek and elegant.

03. Light it up. Don't be afraid of scale! One of my favorite hacks in open-concept kitchens is to go big with lighting. In this kitchen, I opted for oversized dome lights over the island. They cast warm light across the island top and make a bold style statement.

04. Watch your step. I placed a runner on the floor in between the island and the wall. Don't be afraid of color! A colorful rug is a terrific way to bring personality into the room. Be sure to choose a durable fiber with nonslip backing—ideally washable.

05. Accessorize. I chose bar chairs with colorful upholstery to make a bold style statement. If you have a blank wall, use it to hang art, cutting boards, or aprons.

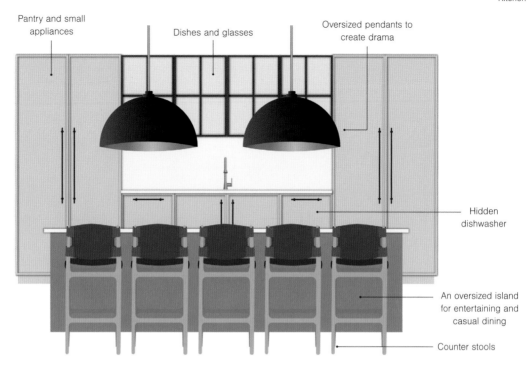

Pantry and small appliances

Dishes and glasses

Oversized pendants to create drama

Hidden dishwasher

An oversized island for entertaining and casual dining

Counter stools

Where the magic happens

At least an 18" overhang for comfy stools at the end

Spices and cooking tools

Cooking utensils and oils

Pots, pans, and serveware

Bakeware, sheet pans, and essentials

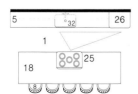

**THE COMFORTABLE TYPE**

Seats 6–8 people

11' W x 14' D

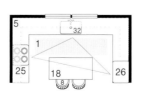

**OPEN & AIRY**

Seats 6–8 people

12' W x 15' D

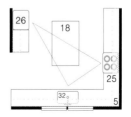

**MADE FOR ENTERTAINMENT**

Seats 10–12 people

14' W x 16' D

# Kitchen Refresh

Looking for a kitchen upgrade that doesn't require an overhaul? With a little elbow grease, some simple tools, and a few replacements, you can give your kitchen a makeover to improve not just its look, but its functionality.

## PAINT YOUR CABINETS

Start with a quick can of paint, or a few! Just remember: semi-gloss paint is best for cabinets to keep them clean and crisp over time.

## SWAP PLUMBING FIXTURES & HARDWARE

Sometimes you just need to swap out fixtures and hardware to work some magic in your room. It's one of the quickest fixes out there, instant gratification guaranteed!

164

## NEW BACKSPLASH & COUNTERTOPS

Countertops and backsplash go a long way for older kitchens. They can drastically change the look and feel of a space.

## CHANGE LIGHTING

Lighting updates and upgrades require professional help, but will bring your kitchen to the next level.

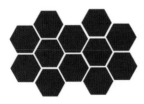

## REPLACE FLOORING

Update your kitchen flooring; something large format works great for cleanability! Less grout = less cleaning.

## UPGRADE YOUR APPLIANCES

Appliances do not have to be boring and they certainly don't all have to match, but they do have to function! This might be on your lowest priority, or your highest, but it's definitely worth exploring.

# What to Do with the Space above Upper Cabinets

It's that age-old question... Many kitchen cabinets don't extend to the ceiling, leaving space that's often overlooked. You can use this space for extra storage or to display artwork, plants, or personal treasures.

### LAYER ARTWORK

Fill an empty space with your personality and showcase things you love through art.

### ADD EXTRA STORAGE WITH BASKETS

Baskets are great for extra storage up top; but try to find ones with lids to protect things inside. It does get quite dusty and greasy up there.

### PLANT BABIES TO THE RESCUE

Real plants with low light needs will love it up on top of cabinets, but if watering seems to be too much of a hassle, fake plants will do just the trick.

### BOOKS & COLLECTIBLES

This space is great for the things you aren't using every day. Cookbooks and some of your favorite collectibles will do great above your cabinetry.

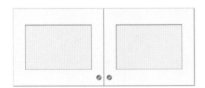

### CLOSE IT UP

If you have room for it, add an extra cabinet on top. It's essentially just a box with doors!

### MIX & MATCH

Take a few of your favorites and layer elements in groups of odd numbers. Remember that tall objects need to be balanced with medium and short objects to feel balanced.

# CHAPTER NINE

# Bedrooms

What's a bedroom? A place where you sleep, right? Well. . . sort of. Although many sleep experts recommend reserving your bedroom for sleep and only sleep, a bedroom can be much more than a place to get your Zzzs. When I design bedrooms, I like to optimize the space to make room for other relaxing pursuits, such as reading, meditating, or just enjoying a quiet cup of tea.

The recipes in this section show how to maximize your space while providing a refuge from the chaos and stress of everyday living. I'll start by walking you through the basics of bedroom design with the Primary Bedroom recipe, before moving on to recipes for a nursery, kid's bedroom, guest bedroom, and hybrid home office/guestroom.. I'll break down the key pieces you'll need to create a fully functional and beautiful space. To help you stay organized, you'll find information and diagrams on storage options and closet systems. And, of course, we'll discuss how to create a peaceful oasis with lighting, accessories, and window treatments.

Before you get started, be sure to refer back to the Function chapter on page 14 to help you think through your particular habits and needs.

167

# Primary Bedroom

Your bedroom should be your oasis—a place to retreat for relaxation and quiet time. Before you get started, look around your space and dream a little bit. Do you have room for a little reading nook? Or perhaps space for a plush cushion or area rug for meditating and stretching? Or maybe just a designated spot to escape the chaotic world for a little while and just relax.

## What You Need:

| | |
|---|---|
| (1) Bed | (1) Dresser |
| (2) Nightstands | (1) Area Rug: 6' x 9', 8' x 10', or 10' x 12' |
| (1) Layered Window Treatment (See Page 68) | (1) Hamper |
| (1) Mirror: 36" Round or Floor-Length | (1) Chandelier |

## Add-Ons:

| | |
|---|---|
| (1) Bench | (1–2) Accent Chair(s) |
| (1) Side Table | (1) Floor Lamp or Table Lamp |
| (1) Ottoman | (1) Bookcase OR Floating Shelves |
| (4) Artworks: 25" x 25" | (1) Artwork: 16" x 20" |
| (2) Artworks: 20" x 30" | (1) Artwork: 24" x 36" |
| (2–3) Euro Throw Pillows or (1) Lumbar Pillow | (2) Medium Plants and (2) Small Plants |

01. Assess your space. How much room do you have? Refer to your floor plan or sketch things out if that's helpful. Your sketch doesn't have to be perfect, and it will help you envision which elements will work for your particular space.

02. Choose the core components. Find balance. Look for furniture that's in proportion to the other furniture and the room itself.

    NIGHTSTAND: Proportion is especially important for nightstands. Wider nightstands work best for larger beds. If you have a king or California king bed, you'll want larger nightstands for balance. Conversely, you don't want to dwarf a smaller bed with huge nightstands. If you have a twin or full bed, look for narrow nightstands. You might even consider a wall-mounted shelf in especially small spaces.

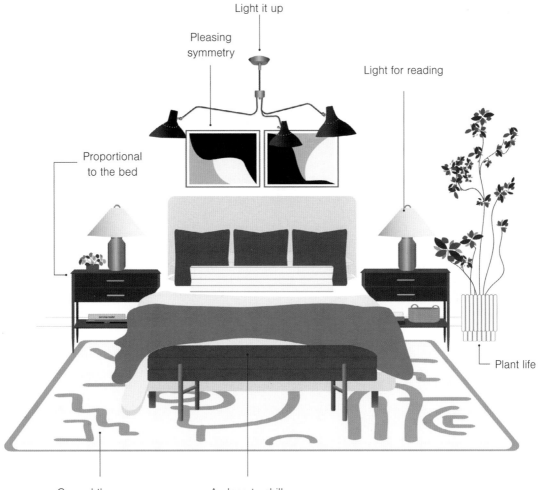

Light it up

Pleasing symmetry

Light for reading

Proportional to the bed

Plant life

Ground the space

A place to chill

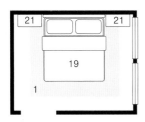

**REST, REST, REST**

10' W x 13' D

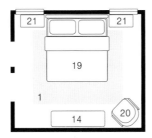

**INTIMATE OASIS**

12' W x 14' D

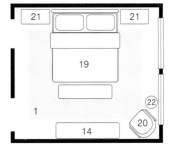

**SPACE TO RELAX**

14' W x 16' D

For this bedroom, I chose nightstands with a wide, low profile to balance the width of the king-size bed.

**DRESSER**: As with nightstands, proportion is an important factor. A wide dresser complements a long wall, while a tall, narrow dresser complements a narrow wall. When I work with a wide dresser, I often like to set two framed art pieces on top to create height.

03. Light it up. I like to have many lighting options in a bedroom.

**OVERHEAD LIGHTING**: Most rooms feature overhead flush mount lighting, which can be harsh on the eyes. You can soften a flush mount light with a shade, or you can replace the fixture with a semi-flush mount light. There are so many stylish and reasonably priced options available. I chose a modern chandelier that hangs from the center of the ceiling, casting light over the entire room.

**BEDSIDE LAMPS**: Table lamps provide lots of options for lighting and help set the mood. Look for lamps with a narrow base to allow room for a book, drinking glass, and other essential items. It's also important to make sure the lamp casts light that's bright enough to read by, but not too bright. If you're dealing with small bedside tables, you might consider wall-mounted bedside lamps. I'm particularly fond of swing arm wall sconces, because you can position the light exactly where you want it.

**FLOOR LAMP OR TABLE LAMP**: If you're lucky enough to have space for a reading nook, you'll want a lamp with enough height to cast light to read by. Depending on your space, you can choose an adjustable floor lamp or go with a table lamp if you have a side table. For the reading nook in this bedroom, I placed an adjustable standing lamp next to one of the chairs for comfortable reading.

**WINDOW COVERINGS**: To give yourself plenty of options for day or night, I recommend layered window treatments with both blackout and sheer options. This allows you to block out light when you're sleeping, but leaves plenty of natural light the rest of the day. Notice how I hung the curtain panels a few inches above the top sash of the window. This creates the illusion of higher ceilings!

04. Create your relaxation zone. If you have enough space, create a zone for relaxation. You can fashion a meditation nook by placing a cushion or pouf in a corner. The same goes for a reading nook. If you have room for a chair and side table, look for a chair that's comfortable enough to curl up in and a side table with a drawer for extra storage. .

05. Watch your step. You'll want a soft rug that will be kind to your bare feet. For this room, I chose a medium-pile rug and centered it underneath the bed, nightstands, and bench.

06. Accessorize. I love decor that both elevates a space and serves an important function. For instance, plants bring nature into your room, which has a calming effect and generates oxygen. I like to use trays and boxes on top of a dresser as catchalls to keep smaller items organized and tidy. Pillows and throws can do double duty, providing both comfort and color.

▶ **PRO TIP**: Need more places to stash your stuff? Consider placing a storage bench or ottoman at the end of your bed to provide handy storage and convenience when putting on shoes or laying out your clothes for the next day. I also recommend bedside tables with drawers or built-in shelving.

Add depth with layered window treatments

Accessorize

Light up the night

Plant baby

Drop your mug or book off

Pull up and put your feet up

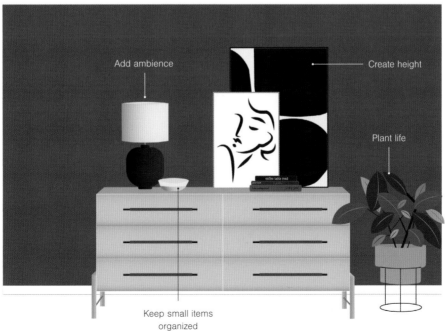

Add ambience

Create height

Plant life

Keep small items organized

# Nursery

Planning for a nursery in your home? First things first: congratulations! This recipe will show you how to create a welcoming room with lots of built-in flexibility, so as the baby grows, you can easily adapt the space for your little one's changing needs. I'll show you how to choose furniture that will work during infant, toddler, and early childhood years. If you're designing for older kids, the Kid's Bedroom recipe builds on the core components of this Nursery recipe.

## What You Need:

| | |
|---|---|
| (1) Convertible Crib | (1) Comfy Chair |
| (1) Side Table | (1–2) Storage Ottoman(s)/Extra Seating |
| (1) Dresser or Changing Table | (1) Area Rug: 5' x 8', 6' x 9', or 8' x 10' |
| (1) Layered Window Treatment (See Page 68) | (3–4) Baskets |
| (1) Hamper | (1) Diaper Pail |
| (1) Floor-Length Mirror | (2) Sconces or Semi-Flush Mount |

## Add-Ons:

| | |
|---|---|
| Accent Wall Detailing (See Page 72) | (1) Bookcase or Floating Shelves |
| (1) Daybed or Trundle Bed | (4) Artworks: 25" x 25" |
| (1) Ottoman | (1) Artwork: 10" x 12" |
| (3) Artworks: 16" x 20" | (1) Reading Lamp |
| (1) Artwork: 8" x 10" | (2) Small Plants |
| (2) Medium Plants | |

01.  Assess your space. How much room do you have? Refer to your floor plan or sketch things out if that's helpful. Your sketch doesn't have to be perfect, and it will help you envision which elements will work for your particular space.

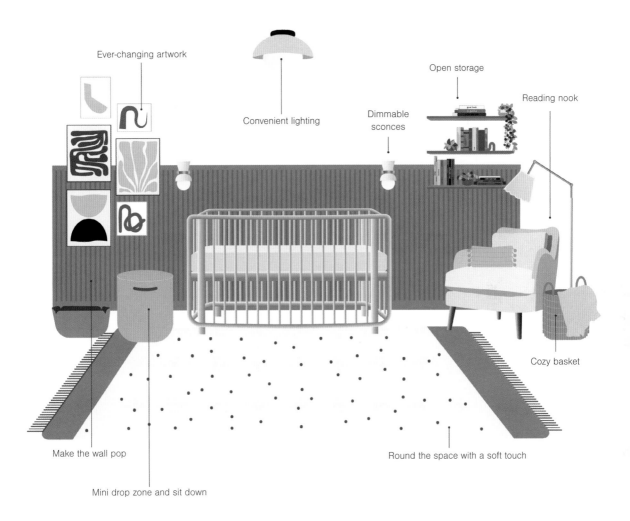

Ever-changing artwork

Convenient lighting

Dimmable sconces

Open storage

Reading nook

Cozy basket

Make the wall pop

Round the space with a soft touch

Mini drop zone and sit down

**COZY UP**

10' W x 10' D

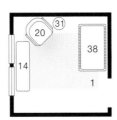

**INTIMATE OASIS**

11' W x 12' D

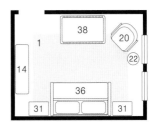

**SPACE TO RELAX**

13' W x 12' D

02.   Choose the core components. Look for pieces that will work for you in the long term and serve more than one purpose. I chose a crib that converts to a toddler bed and eventually a full-size bed. You can use the dresser top with a baby changing tray for a changing station and use the drawers to store clothes and toys. The daybed can double as a couch. (If you do use a dresser as a changing station, please remember, safety first! Be sure to follow the instructions for securely fastening the baby changing tray to the table, and be sure to keep one hand on your baby at all times when using it.)

03.   Organize. Wall-mounted shelves create extra space to store baby essentials, such as a baby monitor, books, and small toys. In this nursery, the storage ottomans next to the crib and changing table provide places to stow blankets, swaddles, and extra linens. Of course, you'll need a hamper with easy access, and I like to keep a roomy basket next to the chair for throw blankets and nursing pillows.

04.   Light it up! Young children are notorious for knocking things over and tearing stuff down. It's best to avoid floor lamps or table lamps. Instead, I recommend a flush mount overhead light and mounted sconces with dimmers. For the window treatment, it's best to avoid curtains. I cannot tell you how many clients tell me their kids pull down curtains! Opt for heavy-duty shades that can block out light so baby can nap.

05.   Pop a squat. Comfortable seating is so important in a nursery. You'll want a cozy chair for reading and feeding time. The ottomans offer extra storage while also providing spots to sit during playtime. If you have room, I suggest a daybed against one wall that works for extra seating, a spot to rest during those late nights, and a place for a sleepover down the road.

06.   Watch your step. A soft rug is essential for playtime and learning to walk, but assume it will get messy! For this reason, I highly recommend a washable rug. Even if you have wall-to-wall carpeting, layering a washable rug on top will save you many headaches down the road.

07.   Accessorize. Here's the fun part. Choose picture frames that are easy to swap art in and out of as your child's interests change. I like to use blankets and throw pillows to add color and texture to the room. Look for washable fabrics made of natural fibers.

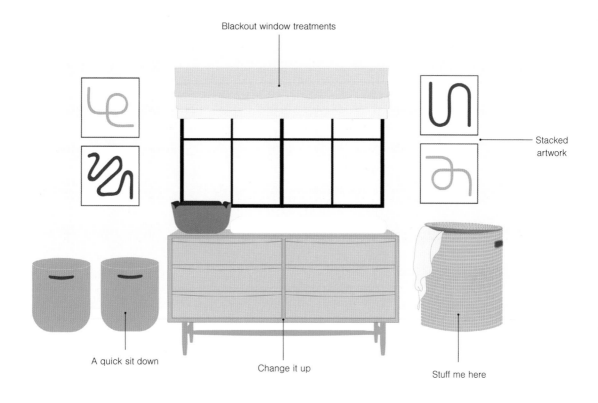

Blackout window treatments

Stacked artwork

A quick sit down

Change it up

Stuff me here

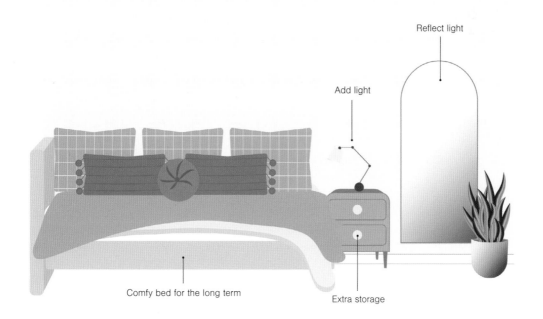

Reflect light

Add light

Comfy bed for the long term

Extra storage

# Kid's Bedroom

Designing a kid's bedroom is all about flexibility. And of course, functionality. Because whatever your child needs and loves right now will change as they grow. Playtime becomes homework time and favorite cartoons become favorite bands. The aim here is to choose furniture and decor that both allows them to express themselves and that can serve different purposes over time. This will allow you to create a more sustainable design for the long term.

## What You Need:

| | |
|---|---|
| (1) Twin or Full Bed | (1–2) Nightstand(s) |
| (1) Desk | (1) Desk Chair |
| (3–4) Baskets | ((1) Area Rug: 5' x 8', 6' x 9', or 8' x 10' |
| (1) Layered Window Treatment (See Page 68) | (1) Open Shelving for Books and Toys |
| (1) Hamper | (1) Floor-Length Mirror |
| (2) Sconces or Semi-Flush Mount | (1) Standing Lamp and (1) Table Lamp |

## Add-Ons:

| | |
|---|---|
| Accent Wall Detailing (See Page 72) | (1) Daybed or Trundle Bed |
| (1) Comfy Chair | (1) Dresser |
| (1–2) Storage Ottoman(s)/Extra Seating | (1) Bulletin Board or Pegboard |
| (1) Floor Lamp or Table Lamp | (1) Bookcase |
| (4) Artworks: 25" x 25" | (3) Artworks: 16" x 20" |
| (1) Artwork: 10" x 12" | (1) Artwork: 8" x 10" |
| (1) Artwork: 10" x 10" | (2) Medium Plants and (2) Small Plants |

01. Assess your space. How much room do you have? Refer to your floor plan or sketch things out if that's helpful. Your sketch doesn't have to be perfect, and it will help you envision which elements will work for your particular space. Check out the Nursery recipe for some basics! Even if you're beyond the nursery stage, many of the pieces in the nursery can work in the Kid's Room.

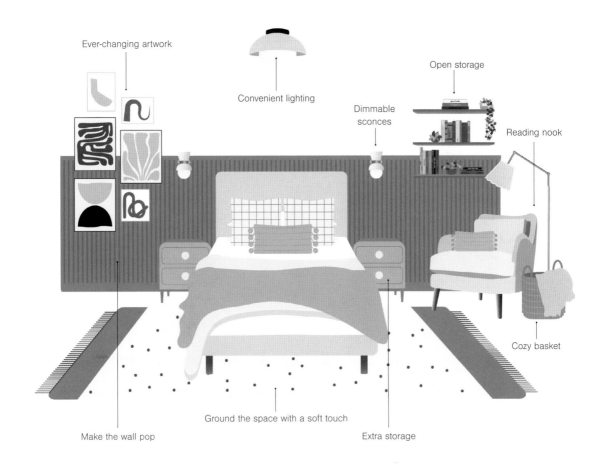

Ever-changing artwork

Convenient lighting

Dimmable sconces

Open storage

Reading nook

Cozy basket

Ground the space with a soft touch

Make the wall pop

Extra storage

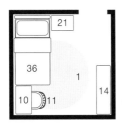

**COZY UP**

10' W x 10' D

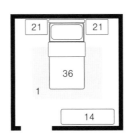

**INTIMATE OASIS**

11' W x 12' D

**SPACE TO RELAX**

13' W x 12' D

02. Choose the core components. Look for pieces that will work for you in the long term. I chose a full-size bed with a headboard and stain-resistant fabric. The nightstands are on the smaller side and proportional to the size of the bed. The desk and chair are lightweight and easy to move around so they can serve different purposes.

03. Organize. The wall-mounted shelves create extra space to store electronics, books, and small toys. You may recognize the storage ottomans, baskets, and hamper from the Nursery recipe. These are just a few examples of items that can transition from stage to stage in your child's life. I placed low open shelves beneath the window and used open baskets as catchalls to keep clutter at bay.

04. Light it up! Because kids use their rooms to sleep, play, and study, I recommend using a variety of lighting fixtures. In this recipe, I used a flush mount light and mounted sconces above the nightstands. I placed a standing lamp next to the chair in the reading nook and a desk lamp for task lighting in the study zone. For the window treatment, I opted for heavy-duty blackout shades.

05. Pop a squat. The cozy chair provides a comfy spot for reading while the ottomans offer extra storage and provide spots to sit. I chose a lightweight desk chair that's easy to scooch in and out from under the desk.

06. Watch your step. A soft rug makes for a great surface to get down on the floor and play. Plan on it getting messy! For this reason, I highly recommend a washable rug. Even if you have wall-to-wall carpeting, layering a washable rug on top will save you many headaches down the road.

07. Accessorize. Here's where you and your child can get creative. In this room, I placed a large bulletin board next to the desk and arranged six different-sized picture frames next to the bed. The frames are easy to open up so you can swap art in and out as your child's interests change. The bulletin board lets kids express themselves over time without needing to redesign the whole room. The large mirror next to the desk reflects light and I added a little plant in a sturdy pot to bring some nature into the room. Throw blankets and pillows in fun colors add some punch and, like the other accessories in the room, they're easy to change as your child's tastes change.

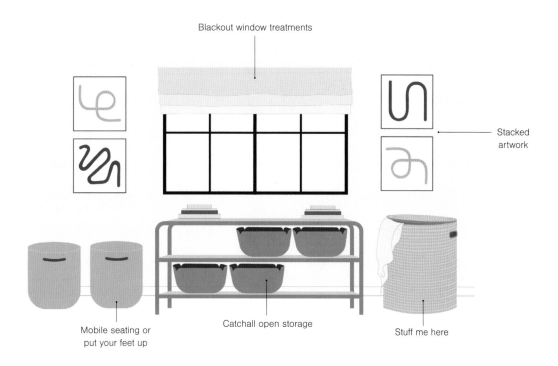

Blackout window treatments

Stacked artwork

Mobile seating or put your feet up

Catchall open storage

Stuff me here

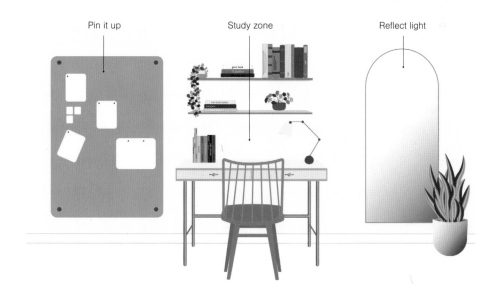

Pin it up

Study zone

Reflect light

# Guest Bedroom

The secret to creating a comfortable, welcoming guest room is to design for flexibility. Your guests will use the room for much more than sleep. They'll use it relax, catch up on work, and take some quiet time away from the rest of the household. When you're designing your guest room, put yourself in the mindset of the guest—what will they want and need in their "home away from home"? This recipe has a light and airy look. The open console, open bed frame, and light sconces mounted above the nightstands all contribute to the open feel, which creates a sense of calm and peace.

## What You Need:

| | |
|---|---|
| (1) Bed | (2) Nightstands |
| (1) Dresser | (1) Open Console |
| (3–4) Baskets | (1) Area Rug: 5' x 8', 6' x 9', or 8' x 10' |
| (1) Side Table | (1) Comfy Chair |
| (1) Layered Window Treatment (See Page 68) | (1) Mirror: 36" Round, or Floor-Length |
| (2) Sconces | Flushmount or Semi-Flush Mount |

## Add-Ons:

| | |
|---|---|
| (1) TV | (1–2) Luggage Storage Stool(s) |
| (1) Basket/Catchall Space | (1) Bench |
| (1) Floor Lamp or Table Lamp | (1) Ottoman |
| (1) Bookcase or Floating Shelves | (1) Artwork: 30" x 40" |
| (2–3) Euro Throw Pillows or (1) Lumbar Pillow | (2) Medium Plants and (2) Small Plants |

01. Assess your space. How much room do you have? Refer to your floor plan or sketch things out if that's helpful. Your sketch doesn't have to be perfect, and it will help you envision which elements will work for your particular space.

02. Choose the core components. For this recipe, I chose a bed with an upholstered headboard and medium-sized nightstands in proportion to the size of the bed. Opposite the bed, I placed an open

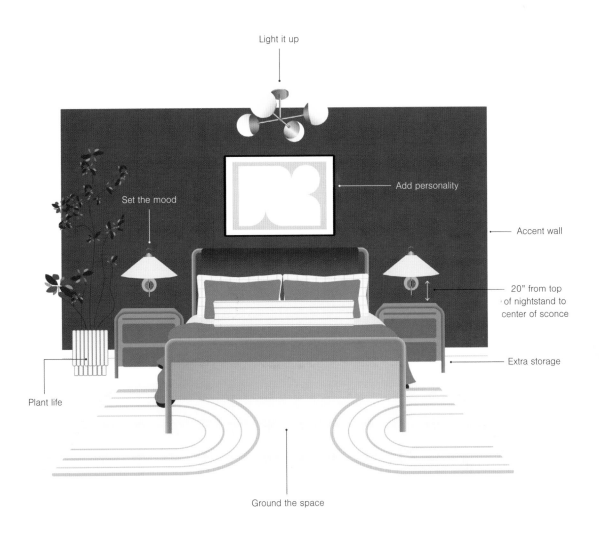

Light it up

Set the mood

Add personality

Accent wall

20" from top of nightstand to center of sconce

Extra storage

Plant life

Ground the space

### REST, REST, REST

10' W x 11' D

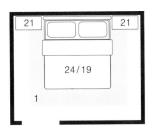

### INTIMATE OASIS

10' W x 12' D

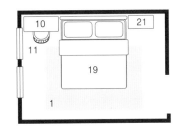

### SPACE TO RELAX

10' W x 14' D

console and tucked folding luggage stools beneath. The tall dresser provides plenty of space for guests to store their items, fits snugly between the two windows, and is proportional to the tall narrow wall. I then created a "chill zone" with a chair paired with a slim side table.

03. Organize. Normally I'm all about storage. But in a guest room, you don't need much—just enough so guests can comfortably store their clothes and stow their luggage away. The dresser and luggage stools do the hard work here and the nightstands have drawers for books, electronic devices, and other items guests may want to keep readily at hand. A catchall basket makes a great place to store extra throw blankets and pillows.

04. Light it up! Because guests will use the rooms to sleep, relax, and catch up on work, I recommend using a variety of lighting fixtures. In this recipe, I used a semi-flush mount light and a standing lamp next to the chair in the "chill zone." The mounted sconces keep the tops of the nightstands clear so guests have plenty of room for their essentials. For the window treatment, I opted for heavy-duty blackout shades paired with soft, sheer curtains so guests can control the level of natural light.

05. Pop a squat. Having a cozy chair can provide a comfy spot for reading and the luggage stools can double as extra seating.

06. Watch your step. To ground the space, I chose an area rug with a bold, graphic pattern beneath the bed. Because this is a low traffic-area, you have more freedom to choose a higher-pile carpet to provide warmth and softness.

07. Accessorize. Because I wanted to keep the room feeling open and airy, I kept the accessories to a minimum. I hung a single, large piece of art above the bed and stacked two smaller framed pieces on top of the dresser. Over the console I mounted a TV, but you may want to opt for another large piece of art or an arrangement of a few different pieces. To bring a calming effect and fresh oxygen to the room, I placed a larger plant in a plant stand on one side of the console and a little potted plant on the side table.

▶ **PRO TIP:** When hanging artwork over a bed, always use French cleats (also called Z-Clips) to keep it extra secure.

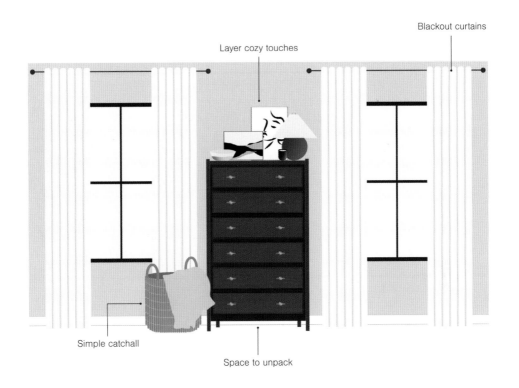

Blackout curtains

Layer cozy touches

Simple catchall

Space to unpack

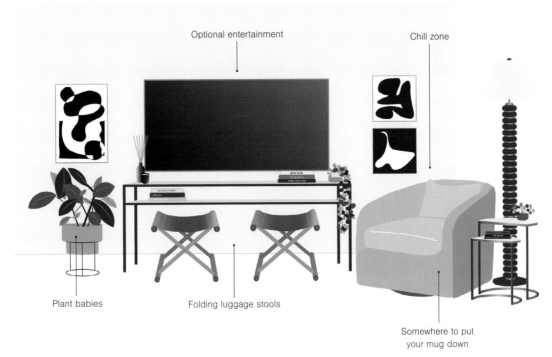

Optional entertainment

Chill zone

Plant babies

Folding luggage stools

Somewhere to put
your mug down

# Multi-Use Bedroom

Is it an office? Or a guest room? It can be both! My advice, though, is to prioritize the office functionality because that's likely how you spend most of your time in the room. In this recipe, I'll share tips and tricks on how to create a fully functioning office that easily doubles as a comfortable, welcoming guest room.

## What You Need:

| | |
|---|---|
| (1) Sleeper Sofa | (1) Desk |
| (1) Chair | (1) Floating Shelf |
| (1) Mirror: 36" Round or Floor-Length | (1) Side Table |
| (1) Laptop Table | (1) Ottoman |
| (1) Area Rug: 5' x 8', 6' Round, 6' x 9', or 8' x 10' | (1) Layered Window Treatment (See Page 68) |
| (1) Floor Lamp and/or (1) Desk Lamp | Semi-Flush Mount |

## Add-Ons:

| | |
|---|---|
| (1) TV | (1–2) Luggage Storage Stool(s) |
| (1) Basket | (1) Bookcase or Floating Shelves |
| (2) Artworks: 20" x 30" | (1) Artwork: 16" x 20" |
| (2–3) Euro Throw Pillows or (1) Lumbar Pillow | (2) Medium Plants and (2) Small Plants |

01. Assess your space. Refer to your floor plan or sketch things out if that's helpful. Your sketch doesn't have to be perfect, and it will help you envision which elements will work for your particular space. Zoning plays a big role in creating a multi-purpose room. Refer back to page 62 for a refresher on creating dedicated spaces in a room.

02. Choose your core components. The secret to success? Make it convertible! Check out the many easily convertible options I chose for the example room in the illustration. The sleeper sofa provides a pleasant video chat background, an extra place to work, and a bed for guests. The mounted monitor can be used as a TV screen for guests. Small side tables give you multiple configurations to use for workspaces or nightstands.

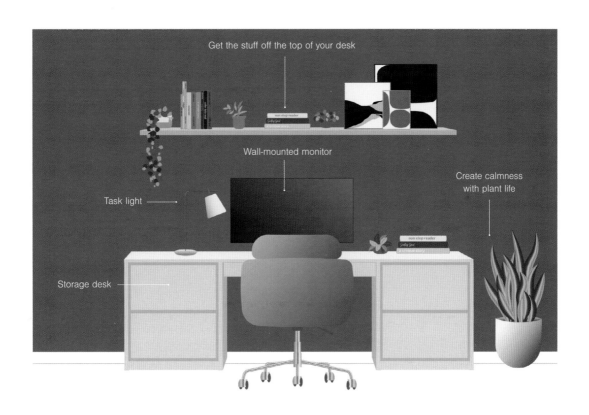

Get the stuff off the top of your desk

Wall-mounted monitor

Task light

Create calmness
with plant life

Storage desk

### MADE FOR TWO

12' W x 10' D

### A GUEST SPACE

13' W x 10' D

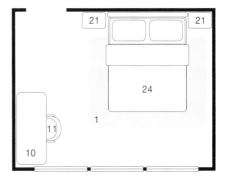

### SPARE BEDROOM

14' W x 10' D

03.   Organize. A multi-use space calls for clever storage and organization systems. I placed a floating shelf above the monitor to help keep the desk area clear of clutter. The desk has deep drawers for files and office supplies. The storage ottoman makes for a perfect place to store guest linens.

04.   Light it up! I like using a variety of lights to meet both office and guestroom needs. The standing lamp next to the couch is adjustable so your guests can use it as a reading light in bed. I set a small lamp on the desk for task lighting and a semi-flush mount fan light provides ambient light and air circulation. A blackout shade paired with sheers give you lots of options—the sheers provide filtered light for all your Zoom calls and the blackout shades keep glare off your screen.

05.   Pop a squat. All of the seating in the room should do double duty for work and relaxing. Getting an office chair that's cushioned will make it comfortable for both office tasks and relaxing. When you get tired of sitting at your desk, you can move to the couch and use the handy mobile laptop table for your workspace. An ottoman provides additional seating (and storage).

06.   Watch your step. To add texture, color, and warmth, I chose a circular area rug that provides a counterpoint to the many square and rectangle shapes in the room.

07.   Accessorize. Because this hardworking room can easily accumulate clutter, I recommend keeping the accessories to a minimum. To create a calming environment, I chose three plants of different sizes that breathe life into the room. I specifically chose a tall plant to balance out the tall window. I hung a large rectangular piece of art between the plant and the window and hung two framed pieces above the sleeper sofa. To lend the room softness, I scattered several pillows of different sizes on the couch. These add color and texture and can easily be swapped around for a room refresh.

Functional lighting

Accent lighting

The perfect Zoom call background

Sleeper sofa

Put your mug down

Mobile laptop table

Move me around and put your feet up

Ground the space

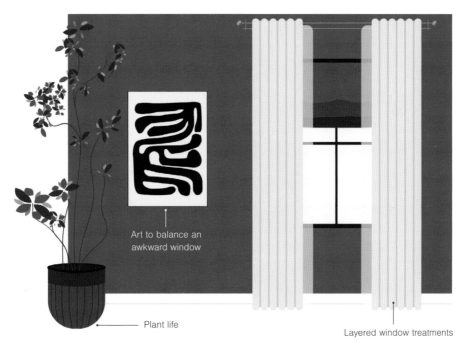

Art to balance an awkward window

Plant life

Layered window treatments

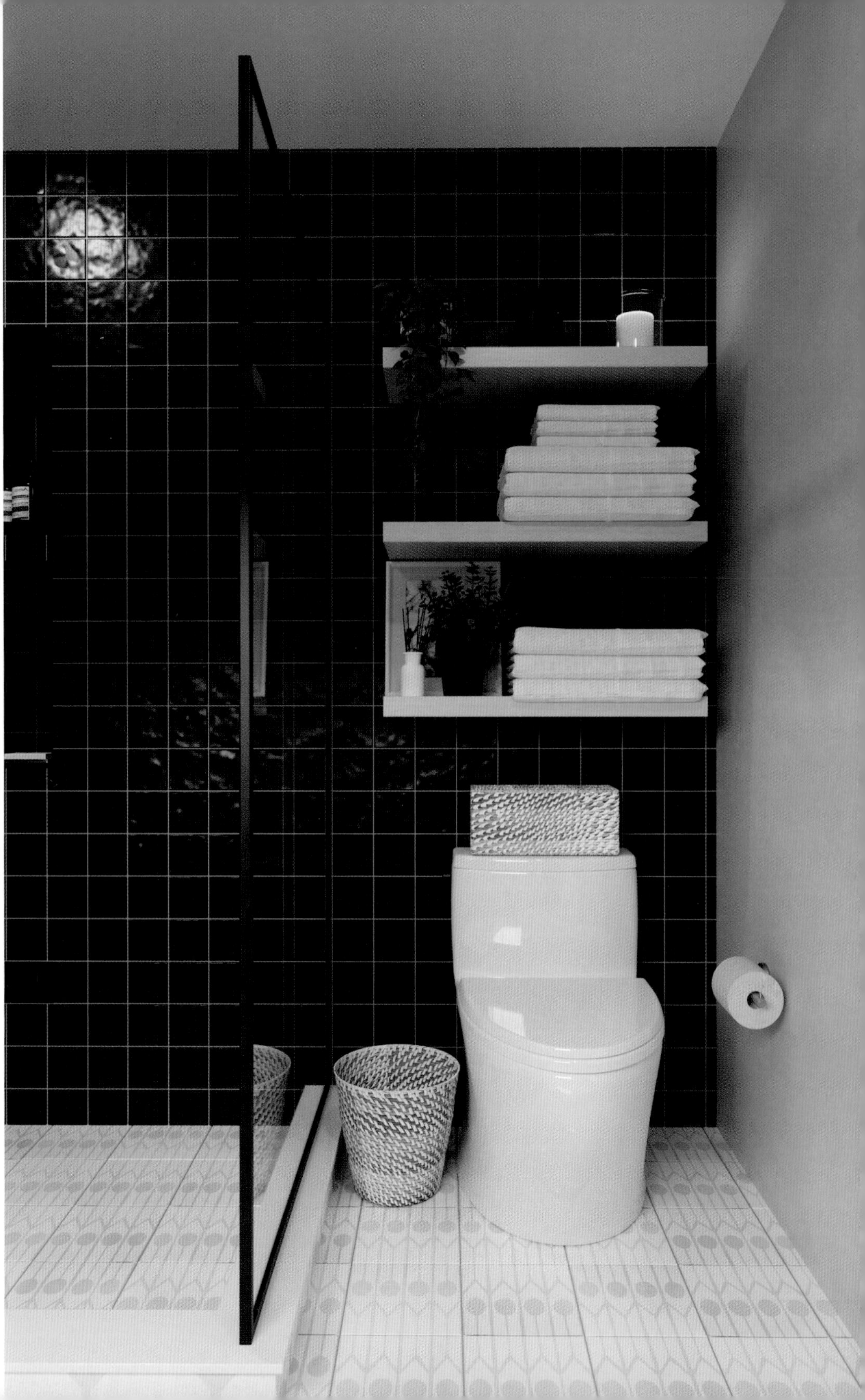

# CHAPTER TEN

# Bathrooms

Okay, so the bathroom may not be the most exciting room in the house. But that doesn't mean we should overlook its potential. After all, we spend a lot of time there. . . we're talking two full years over the course our lives! Why not make it a pleasant experience? Whether you're working with a tiny powder room or a spacious en suite bathroom, you'll find plenty of inspiration and solutions in these pages. I've pulled together everything you need to know to create a stylish bathroom that not only serves practical purposes but also feels like a restful refuge from the world.

# Powder Room

Half bathrooms, often called powder rooms, provide the perfect opportunity to make a bold statement. You could paint the walls a deep shade, put up boldly patterned wallpaper, or lay down colorful tile. Let your creative energy flow!

Because this sort of bathroom will likely be used by both you and your guests, consider their needs and provide any essentials that will make them comfortable—tissues, hand sanitizer, aromatic spray, etc.

## What You Need:

| | |
|---|---|
| (1) Toilet | (1) Mirror or Medicine Cabinet |
| (1) Vanity | (1) Overhead Scone or (2) Side Mount Sconces |
| (1) Faucet | (1) Semi-Flush Mount or Flush Mount |
| Unique Wall Treatment | (1) Hand Towel Holder |
| (1) Toilet Paper Holder | (1) Trash Can |

## Add-Ons:

| | |
|---|---|
| (1) Bathmat or Runner | (1) Artwork: 24" W x 36" H |
| (1) Basket | (1) Semi-Transparent Roman or Roller Shade |

01. Assess your space. Refer to your floor plan or sketch things out if that's helpful. Your sketch doesn't have to be perfect, and it will help you envision which elements will work for your particular space.

02. Choose your core components. For the simple and sophisticated powder room shown opposite, I chose a narrow vanity that fits the wall, leaving just a few inches of space on either side.

03. Organize! The drawers in the vanity provide space for extra toilet paper, soap, and hand towels. I hung a floating shelf above the toilet for a convenient place to set things.

04. Light it up. In this powder room, I hung a semi-flush mount light overhead for ambient light and positioned two wall sconces on the side of the mirror, which reflects the warm light.

05. Accessorize. In this powder room, I painted the walls a dark shade for a moody look. Then I hung a bold graphic framed print above the toilet for contrast, and a floating shelf to store things.

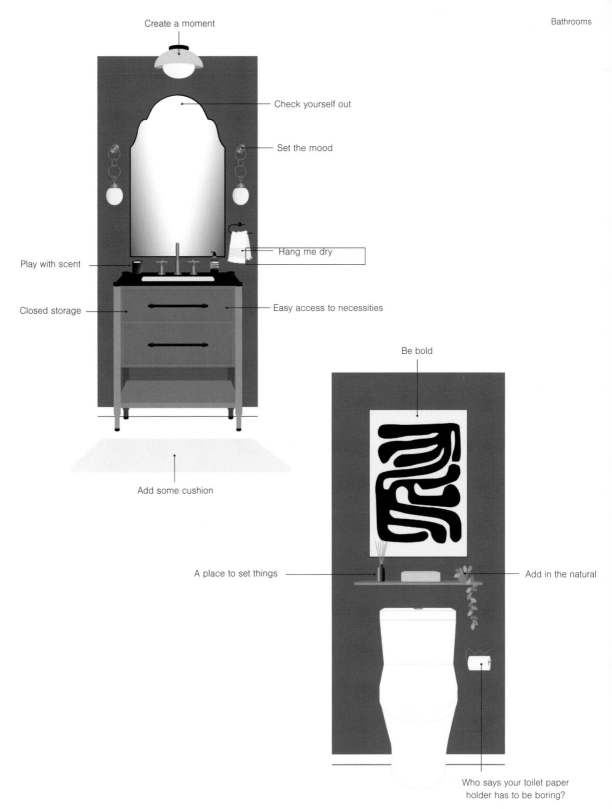

Create a moment

Check yourself out

Set the mood

Hang me dry

Play with scent

Closed storage

Easy access to necessities

Add some cushion

Be bold

A place to set things

Add in the natural

Who says your toilet paper holder has to be boring?

# Small Bathroom

You'll be astonished at how much you can do with a small bathroom. It's all about optimizing the space and maximizing your storage capacity. Before you get started, think through your specific bathroom needs. Is this bathroom the only bathroom in the house, or is it one of many? Do you want a spa vibe, or a bright energetic feel?

## What You Need:

| | |
|---|---|
| (1) Toilet | (1) Vanity |
| (1) Faucet | (1) Mirror or Medicine Cabinet |
| (1) Overhead Sconce or (2) Side Mount Sconces | (1) Semi-Flush Mount or Flush Mount |
| Unique Wall Treatment | (1) Tub or Shower |
| (1) Hand Towel Holder | (1) Toilet Paper Holder |
| (2–4) Robe Hooks | (1) Towel Bar |
| (1) Trash Can | |

## Add-Ons:

| | |
|---|---|
| (2–3) Floating Shelves: 24" W x 10–12" D | (1) Basket |
| (1) Linen Cabinet | (1) Heated Towel Bar |
| (1–2) Bath Mat(s) or Runner(s) | (1) Semi-Transparent Roman or Roller Shade |
| (2) Artworks: 24" W x 36" H | |

01. Assess your space. Refer to your floor plan or sketch things out if that's helpful. Your sketch doesn't have to be perfect, and it will help you envision which elements will work for your particular space.

02. Choose your core components. For the bathroom shown opposite, I chose a wall-mounted floating vanity with open space beneath which lends an airy feel to the space.

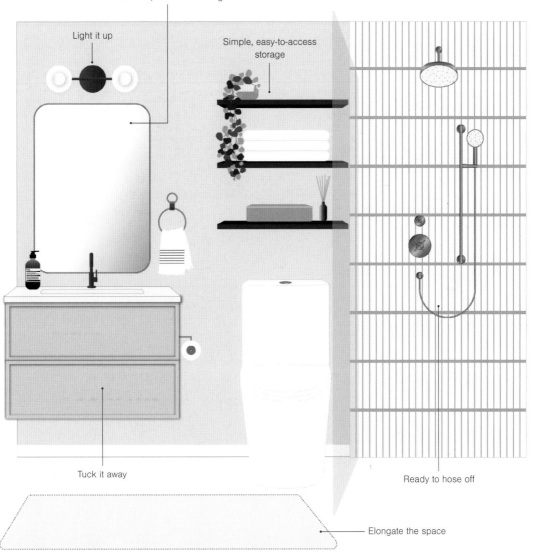

Is it a mirror, or hidden storage?

Light it up

Simple, easy-to-access storage

Tuck it away

Ready to hose off

Elongate the space

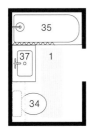

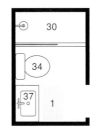

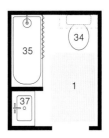

**STACKED FUNCTION**

8' W x 5' D

**A UNIQUE TAKE**

8' W x 8' D

**CLEAN & FOCUSED**

8' W x 5' D

**FULL OF SPACE**

8' W x 7' D

03. Organize! The deep drawers in the vanity provide space for extra toilet paper, soap, and hand towels. I hung three floating shelves above the toilet for simple, easy-to-access storage. The recessed shelves in the shower keep shampoo and soap tucked out of the way. I mounted hooks on the back of the door instead of taking up precious wall space for towel racks.

04. Light it up. I hung a semi-flush mount light overhead that provides ambient light. Then, I positioned sconce lights above the mirror for more focused lighting for your grooming needs.

05. Watch your step. To elongate the space, I chose a rectangular rug that extends across the space in front of the vanity and toilet.

06. Accessorize. I kept it simple and hung two framed pieces on the wall next to the door. If your door opens inward, make sure that the doorknob and towel hooks don't knock into the artwork.

Focus on light

Store those bottles with purpose

Add personality with the illusion of height

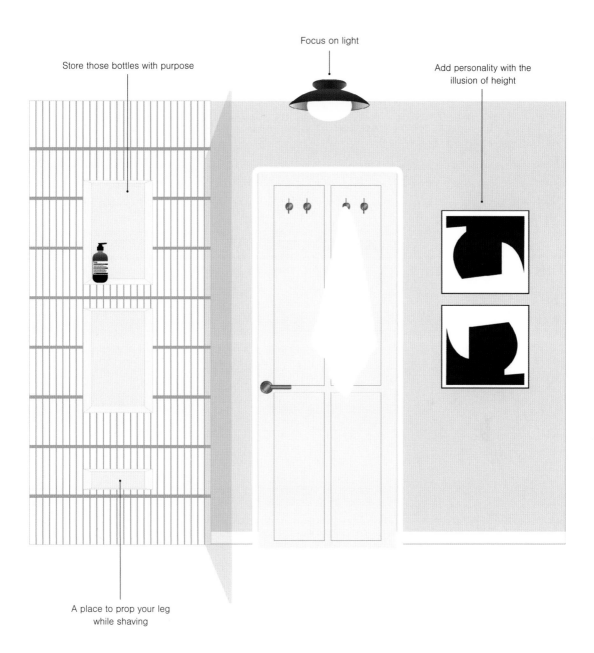

A place to prop your leg while shaving

# Medium Bathroom

Lucky you, you have a bit more space to work with! What can you add to make this bathroom feel more like you? It doesn't have to be an actual "thing." Fewer objects on the countertops makes it easier to keep the space tidy. Maybe it's dramatic lighting, or a shower curtain hung close to the ceiling to make the room feel more elegant? The recipe below works for any of the four floor plans shown.

## What You Need:

(1) Toilet

(1) Single or Double Vanity

(1–2) Faucet(s)

(1–2) Mirror(s) or Medicine Cabinet(s)

(1–2) Overhead Sconce(s)

(1) Semi-Flush Mount or Flush Mount

Unique Wall Treatment

(1) Tub or Shower

(1–2) Hand Towel Holder(s)

(1) Toilet Paper Holder

(4) Robe Hooks

(1–2) Towel Bar(s)

(1) Trash Can

## Add-Ons:

(2–3) Floating Shelves: 24" W x 10–12" D

(1) Linen Cabinet

(1–2) Bath Mat(s) or Runner(s)

(3) Artworks: 24" W x 36" H

(1) Basket

(1) Heated Towel Bar

(1) Semi-Transparent Roman or Roller Shade

01. Assess your space. Refer to your floor plan or sketch things out if that's helpful. Your sketch doesn't have to be perfect, and it will help you envision which elements will work for your particular space.

02. Choose your core components. I went with a double-sink vanity for a casual feel. The width and double sinks provide plenty of space for two to use the room at the same time.

Essential lighting

Create height with oversized mirrors

Create a casual feeling with a vanity that feels like furniture

**ONE OF EVERYTHING**

9' W x 9' D

**DIVISION OF SPACE**

12' W x 6' D

**A SNUG FIT**

8' W x 10' D

**MADE FOR STORAGE**

10' W x 8' D

03.   Organize! The deep drawers in the vanity provide space for extra toilet paper, soap, and hand towels.

04.   Light it up. I hung a semi-flush mount light overhead that provides ambient light. Then, I positioned two sconce lights above the mirrors for more focused light in which to do your grooming. A Roman shade provides privacy and has a clean, tidy look when pulled up or pulled down.

05.   Watch your step. An area rug is one of the best ways to brighten up or add character to the space. For this bathroom, I chose a long rectangular rug. But you could get creative with a few bathmats. Mix and match to make it fun!

06.   Accessorize. I hung two tall mirrors over the vanity and set a sculptural vase with leafy branches in between the sinks. Plants work well in bathrooms to bring in a touch of nature.

Pull in your natural senses and hide away

# Large Bathroom

With a large bathroom, you have the luxury to fit both a shower and a tub, if you'd like. The floor plans I've included for this recipe all feature both, but you could go with just a shower or a tub and use the extra space for a bench or comfy seat. The secret to success in a large bathroom is to layer complementary lighting, wall materials, and flooring to create a cohesive look throughout.

## What You Need:

| | |
|---|---|
| (1) Toilet | (1) Double Vanity or (2) Single Vanities |
| (2) Faucets | (2) Mirrors or Medicine Cabinets |
| (2) Overhead Sconces | (1) Semi-Flush Mount or Flush Mount |
| Unique Wall Treatment | (1) Freestanding Tub |
| (1) Shower | (2) Hand Towel Holders |
| (1) Toilet Paper Holder | (4) Robe Hooks |
| (2) Towel Bars | (1) Trash Can |

## Add-Ons:

| | |
|---|---|
| (2–3) Floating Shelves: 24" W x 10–12" D | (1) Basket |
| (1) Linen Cabinet | (1) Heated Towel Bar |
| (1–2) Bath Mat(s) or Runner(s) | (1) Semi-Transparent Roman or Roller Shade |
| (3) Artworks: 24" W x 36" H | |

01. Assess your space. Refer to your floor plan or sketch things out if that's helpful. Your sketch doesn't have to be perfect, and it will help you envision which elements will work for your particular space.

02. Choose your core components. For the Cohesive Relaxation bathroom I chose a wide double vanity that provides plenty of counter space. The tub is positioned along one of the side walls and I put a partition between the tub and toilet.

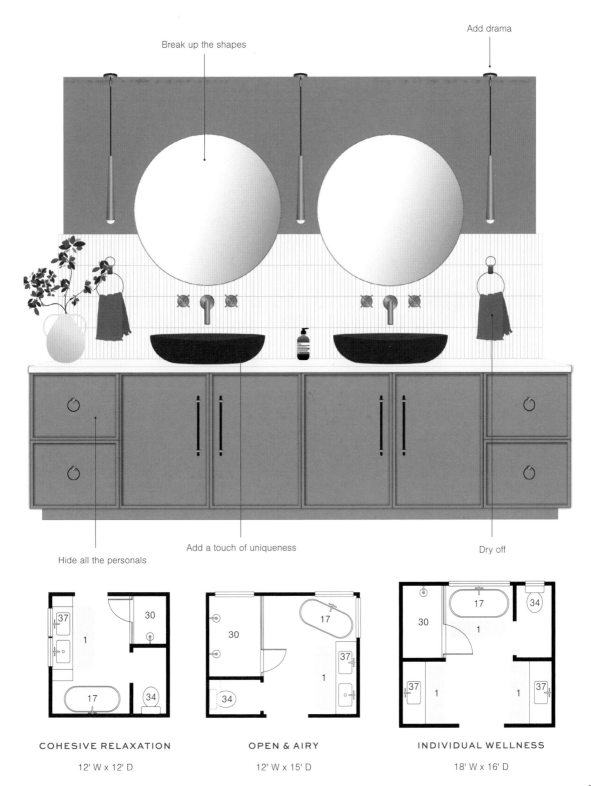

Break up the shapes

Add drama

Hide all the personals

Add a touch of uniqueness

Dry off

**COHESIVE RELAXATION**

12' W x 12' D

**OPEN & AIRY**

12' W x 15' D

**INDIVIDUAL WELLNESS**

18' W x 16' D

03.   Organize! You have room in larger bathrooms for various types of storage. You really can't have too much storage in my opinion. In this bathroom, the combination of cabinets and drawers in the vanity provide ample space to store all your essentials, along with extra towels, bathmats, and washcloths. A shallow built-in shelf behind the tub makes a handy place to set shampoo, soap, and a few decorative items. A lidded basket next to the tub works as either a hamper or a place to store extra towels.

04.   Light it up. In this bathroom, it's all about drama. I hung three pendant lights above the vanity, and the mirrors help reflect the warm light across the room. On the wall above the tub, I hung three sconce lights to cast light downward onto the artwork. For overhead lighting, you could go with a semi-flush mount or flush mount light to provide ambient light for the entire room.

05.   Watch your step. For each of these floor plans I placed a rectangular rug in front of the vanity. You can then mix and match bathmats in front of the tub and toilet.

06.   Accessorize. I hung two round mirrors over the vanity and set a sculptural vase with leafy branches on one side. Next to the tub, I positioned a tall potted plant and set a tray and a few decorative items on the shelf behind the tub.

▶ PRO TIP: Consider smell. Okay, that sounds awkward, but I'm not talking about hiding smells— rather, I'm encouraging good ones! A signature scent can make a bathroom feel welcoming and relaxing. Do you want a fresh-breeze vibe, or a cozy winter feel?

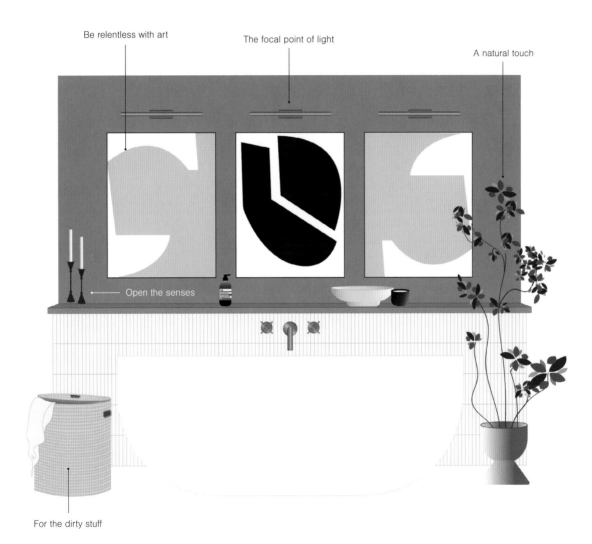

Be relentless with art

The focal point of light

A natural touch

Open the senses

For the dirty stuff

# Kid's Bathroom

A kid's bathroom tends to get messy in record time. That's why clever storage systems are essential. It's also helpful to think long term—you child's needs and tastes will change as they grow. So do what you can to choose elements that will grow and adjust with them. I recommend keeping things neutral and adding color with items that you can easily change out, such as towels, artwork, and baskets.

## What You Need:

| | |
|---|---|
| (1) Toilet | (1) Tub or Shower |
| (1) Single or Double Vanity | (1–2) Hand Towel Holder(s) |
| (1–2) Faucet(s) | (1) Toilet Paper Holder |
| (1–2) Mirror(s) or Medicine Cabinet(s) | (4) Robe Hooks |
| (1–2) Overhead Sconce | (1–2) Towel Bar(s) |
| (1) Semi-Flush Mount or Flush Mount | (1) Trash Can |
| Unique Wall Treatment | |

## Add-Ons:

| | |
|---|---|
| (2–3) Floating Shelves: 24" W x 10–12" D | (1) Basket |
| (1) Linen Cabinet | (1) Semi-Transparent Roman or Roller Shade |
| (1–2) Bath Mat(s) or Runners(s) | (2–3) Artworks: 16" W x 20" H |

01. Assess your space. Refer to your floor plan or sketch things out if that's helpful. Your sketch doesn't have to be perfect, and it will help you envision which elements will work for your particular space.

02. Choose your core components. For the Shared Cohesion bathroom I chose a wide double-sink vanity that provides plenty of counter space. The tub and shower combo features an adjustable showerhead for kids of all sizes. I mounted the shower curtain rod from the ceiling to create height.

03. Organize! In a kid's bathroom, you need plenty of space to stash all sorts of gear. The tall built-in cabinet above the vanity has shelving inside for toothbrushes, toothpaste, and smaller items. The cabinet above the toilet is deeper and has room for extra toilet paper and bath toys. The vanity itself has plenty of drawers for grooming items and roomy cabinets for linens. I mounted a floating

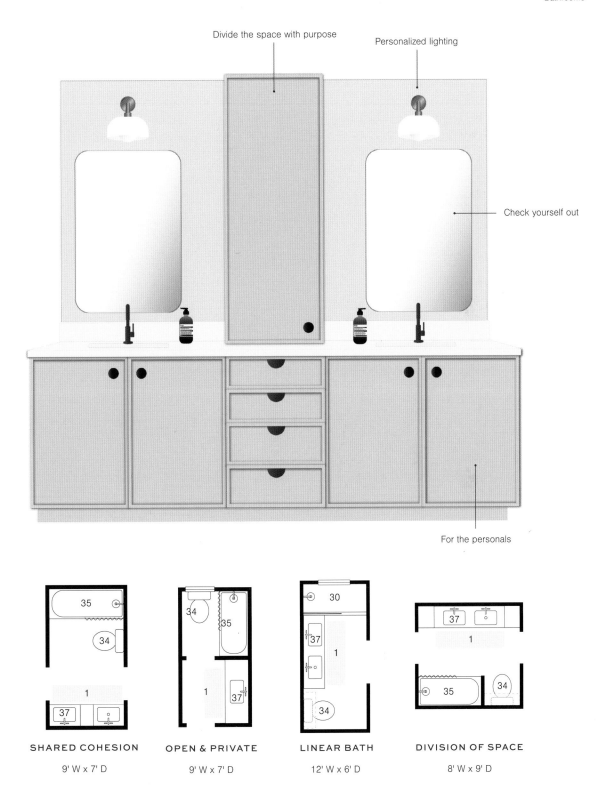

Divide the space with purpose

Personalized lighting

Check yourself out

For the personals

**SHARED COHESION**

9' W x 7' D

**OPEN & PRIVATE**

9' W x 7' D

**LINEAR BATH**

12' W x 6' D

**DIVISION OF SPACE**

8' W x 9' D

shelf above the toilet for essentials. You might consider installing hooks on the back of the door at lower levels to make it easy for kids to hang their towels.

04. Light it up. I opt for more practical lighting in a kid's bathroom. You want to be able to see well when clipping nails and combing hair. I positioned two sconce lights above the mirrors. For overhead lighting, you could go with a semi-flush mount or flush mount light to provide ambient light for the entire room.

05. Watch your step. For each of these floor plans I placed a rectangular rug in front of the vanity. You can then mix and match bathmats in front of the tub and toilet.

06. Accessorize. It's best to keep surface areas clear, so I didn't add much in the way of decorative items. I simply hung two rectangular mirrors over the vanity that reflect the light from the sconces overhead.

Adjustability is everything

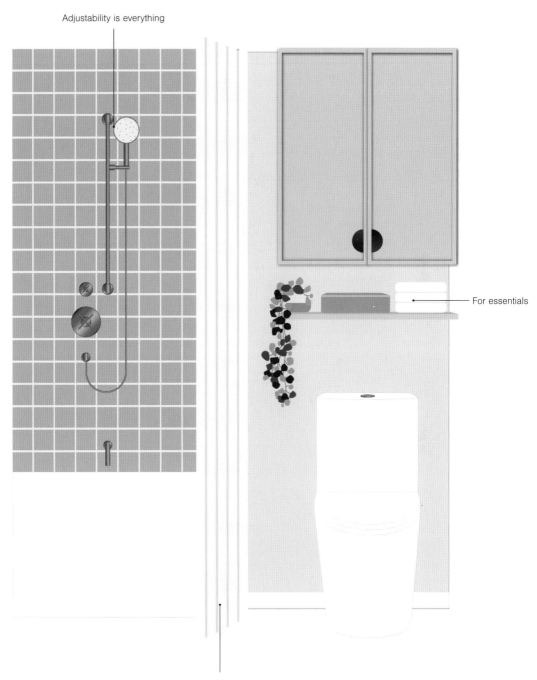

For essentials

Add height by mounting a regular curtain to
the ceiling on the outside of your tub

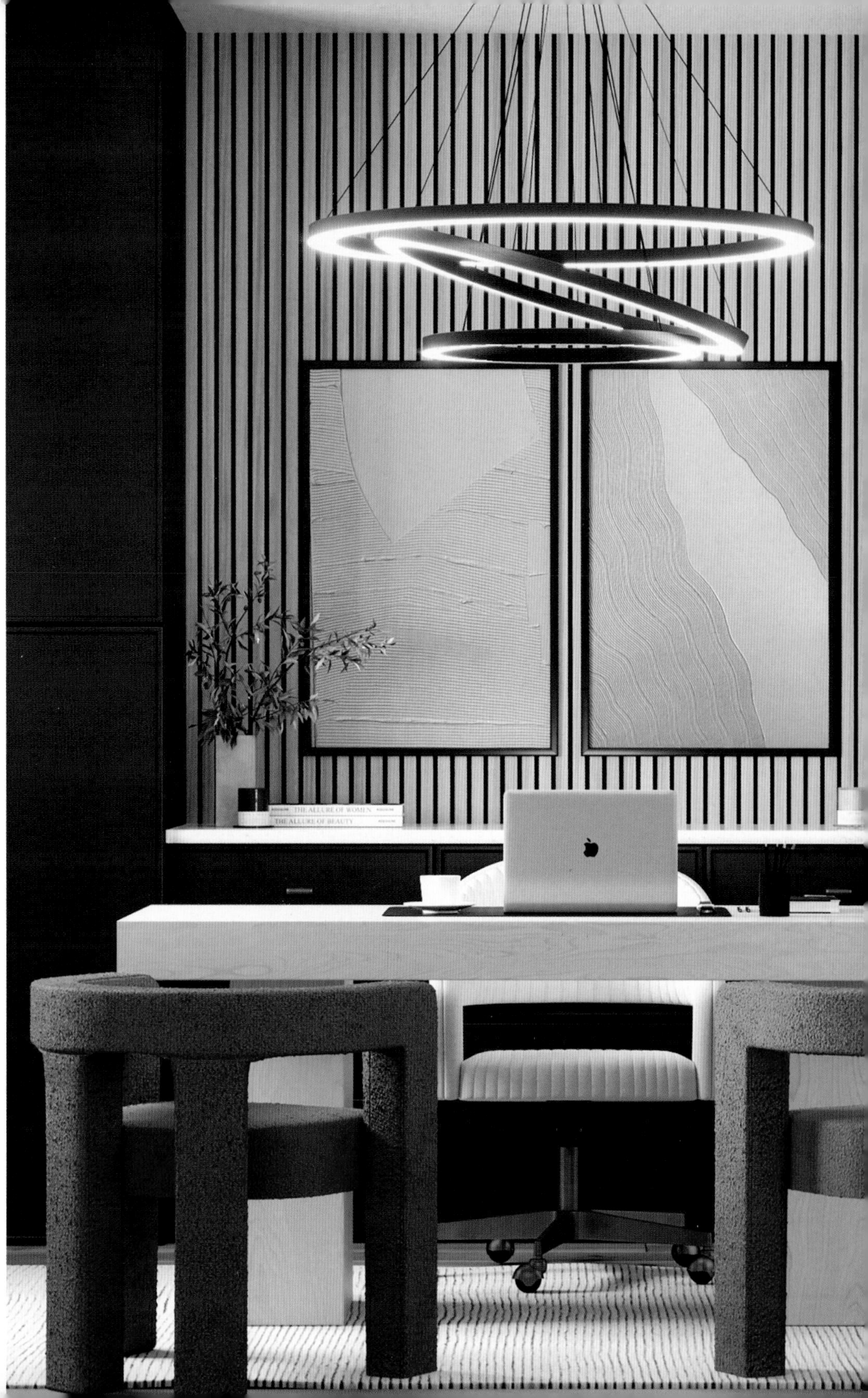
THE ALLURE OF WOMEN
THE ALLURE OF BEAUTY

# CHAPTER ELEVEN

# Home Office

So many of us work from home at least a few days a week. Keep in mind that you don't need a separate room for a home office—you just need a dedicated place to focus with minimal distractions. And ideally your home office will be a space that you look forward to spending time in. This section has recipes for micro offices, big offices, and everything in between! I'll walk you through the key pieces and offer up creative storage solutions to help you maximize your comfort and productivity.

# Micro Office

Don't have a room that you can dedicate to an office? Don't despair. This recipe shows how to make something made from nothing! There's plenty you can do to create a home office in your existing space. This is where zoning comes in (see page 62 for zoning tips). You can zone a closet, an empty wall, or a corner of a room for your office. This recipe offers three different options for different-sized spaces. Take what works for you to create a fully functioning space with an element of fun.

## What You Need:

| Converted Closet<br>6' W x 2' D | Between Things<br>4' W x 2' D | Hidden Corner<br>5' W x 4' D |
|---|---|---|
| (1) Desk: 48–54" W | (1) Desk: 36–48" W | (1) Desk: 30" W |
| (1) Desk Chair | (1) Desk Chair | (1) Bookcase: 30" W |
| (1–2) Bookcase(s) size: 18" W | (2-3) Floating Shelves | (1) Desk Chair |
| (1) Flush Mount | (1) Flush Mount | (1) Flush Mount |
| (1) Desk Lamp | (1) Desk Lamp | (1) Desk Lamp |
| (1) Creative Wall Treatment | (1) Creative Wall Treatment | (1) Creative Wall Treatment |
| (1) Cable Management Tray | (1) Cable Management Tray | (1) Cable Management Tray |
| (1) Cable Management Cord | (1) Cable Management Cord | (1) Cable Management Cord |

## Add-Ons:

| | | |
|---|---|---|
| (2–3) Floating Shelves | Puck or Strip Lights | (2–3) Baskets with Lids |
| (1) Artwork: 8" W x 10" H | (1) Artwork: 10" W x 12" H | (2) Artworks: 16" W x 20" H |
| (1) Small Plant | (1) Medium Plant | (1) Writing Utensil Holder |
| (1) Trash Can | | |

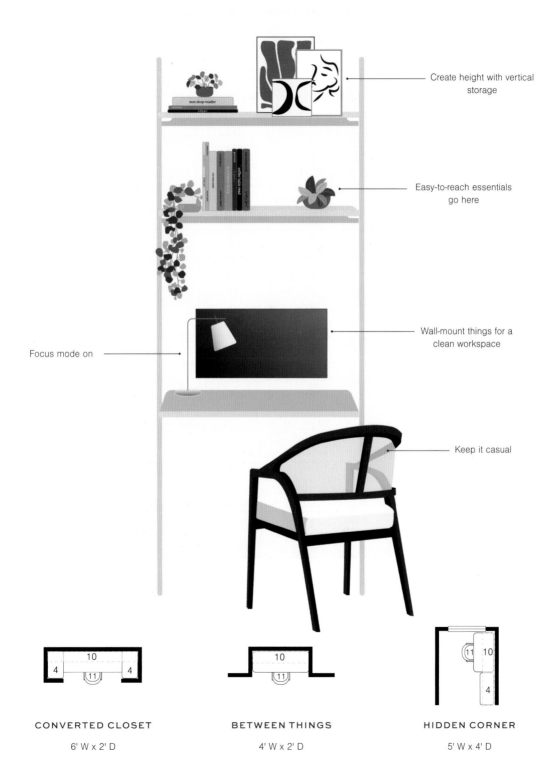

Create height with vertical storage

Easy-to-reach essentials go here

Wall-mount things for a clean workspace

Focus mode on

Keep it casual

**CONVERTED CLOSET**

6' W x 2' D

**BETWEEN THINGS**

4' W x 2' D

**HIDDEN CORNER**

5' W x 4' D

01. Assess your space. Refer to your floor plan or sketch things out if that's helpful. Your sketch doesn't have to be perfect, and it will help you envision which elements will work for your particular space.

02. Choose your core components.

    **CONVERTED CLOSET**: For this tall, narrow space, I chose a combination of an open bookshelf and writing desk. When not at work, you can use the chair for extra seating.

    **BETWEEN THINGS**: In this slightly wider space, I had room for a small open desk and a stylish office chair on wheels.

    **HIDDEN CORNER**: The roomy desk has room beneath to tuck the pedestal filing cabinet to free up floor space.

03. Organize! In small spaces, open shelving works wonders. Baskets with lids make it easy to stash things away and keep your workspace clear.

    **CONVERTED CLOSET**: The open bookshelf maximizes vertical space and makes for easy access to office supplies you need readily at hand. If you have some extra shelf space, you can arrange a few decorative pieces. I mounted the monitor on the wall to free up desk space.

    **BETWEEN THINGS**: I mounted floating shelves above the desk and left plenty of space between the desktop and the first shelf for the computer monitor or open laptop.

    **HIDDEN CORNER**: The pedestal filing cabinet on wheels provides a place for your important papers and offers extra seating for your collaborators.

04. Light it up. In small spaces you'll need focused lighting. Overhead lighting with a flush mount is ideal—but make sure to combine it with task lighting for late work nights. You might also consider adding puck or strip lights under shelving for a luxurious look.

    **CONVERTED CLOSET**: A small lamp sits on the desktop for task lighting, while the ceiling light provides ambient light.

    **BETWEEN THINGS**: A semi-flush mount light directs light onto the desktop, while a table lamp provides more focused task lighting.

    **HIDDEN CORNER**: The adjustable-height floor lamp makes it easy to change your light level throughout the day. The overhead semi-flush mount light directs light onto the desktop.

05. Watch your step. If you have space for an area rug, go for it! But make sure you choose a low-pile option so you can easily slide your chair in and out from your desk.

06. Accessorize. Space is at a premium in these smaller spaces, so I recommend keeping your accessories to a minimum.

07. **CONVERTED CLOSET**: I stacked a few small pieces of framed artwork on the top shelf and tucked a small plant with a trailing vine on the lower shelf. Just a few decorative touches can go a long way in adding personality to your space.

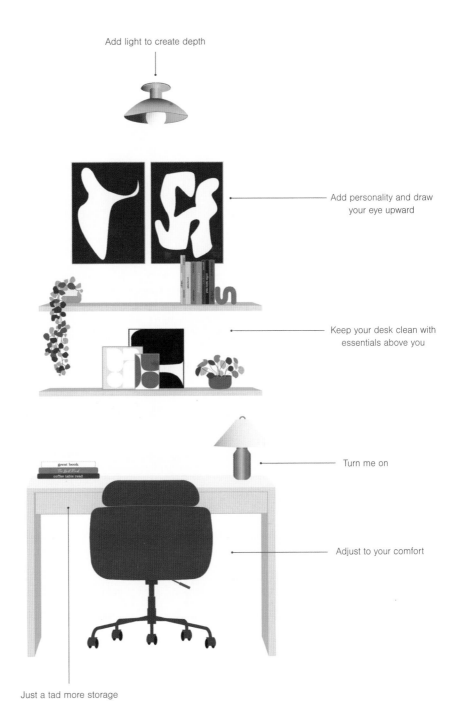

Add light to create depth

Add personality and draw
your eye upward

Keep your desk clean with
essentials above you

Turn me on

Adjust to your comfort

Just a tad more storage

08. **BETWEEN THINGS:** Two framed pieces of art above the top shelf draw the eye upward, creating the feeling of height. I placed a little potted plant and a few books on the top shelf and then arranged some framed photos on the second shelf.

09. **HIDDEN CORNER:** I had more room to play with in this space, so I placed a potted plant to the side of the desk to bring in a natural element. I then hung two rectangular framed pieces of artwork above the desk for a bold focal point.

Draw your eye upward

Lighting with purpose

The things that keep you
motivated and inspired

Mobile storage

Move around, up and down—this
is made for ergonomic lovers

# Small Office

If you have a separate small room for your home office, you can easily create a quiet place to focus. Work can get stressful, so I like to add in hints of nature. I find the more connected to nature I feel, the more relaxed I am. This recipe shows three different configurations in three different-sized spaces. Feel free to pick and choose elements from each to make your office as functional and comfortable as possible.

## What You Need:

| Minimal Works | Professional Feeling | Space to Spread Out |
| --- | --- | --- |
| 7' W x 7' D | 8' W x 8' D | 10' W x 10' D |
| (1) Desk: 60–72" W | (1) Desk: 60" W | (1) L-Shaped Desk: 72" x 72" |
| (1) Desk Chair | (1) Desk Chair | (1) Desk Chair |
| (1) Corner Bookcase: 20" W | (1) Corner Bookcase: 30" W | (2) Bookcases: 36" W |
| (1) Flush Mount | (1) Flush Mount | (1) Flush Mount |
| (1) Desk Lamp | (1) Desk Lamp | (1) Desk Lamp |
| (1) Creative Wall Treatment | (1) Creative Wall Treatment | (1) Creative Wall Treatment |
| (1) Cable Management Tray | (1) Cable Management Tray | (1) Cable Management Tray |
| (1) Cable Management Cord | (1) Cable Management Cord | (1) Cable Management Cord |

## Add-Ons:

| | | |
| --- | --- | --- |
| (2–3) Floating Shelves | Puck or Strip Lights | Roman or Roller Shade |
| (2) Artworks: 16" W x 20" H | (1) Artwork: 8" W x 10" H | (1) Artwork: 10" W x 12" H |
| (1) Medium Plant | (1) Small Plant | (2–3) Baskets with Lids |
| (1) Writing Utensil Holder | (1) Trash Can | |

01. Assess your space. Refer to your floor plan or sketch things out if that's helpful. Your sketch doesn't have to be perfect, and it will help you envision which elements will work for your particular space.

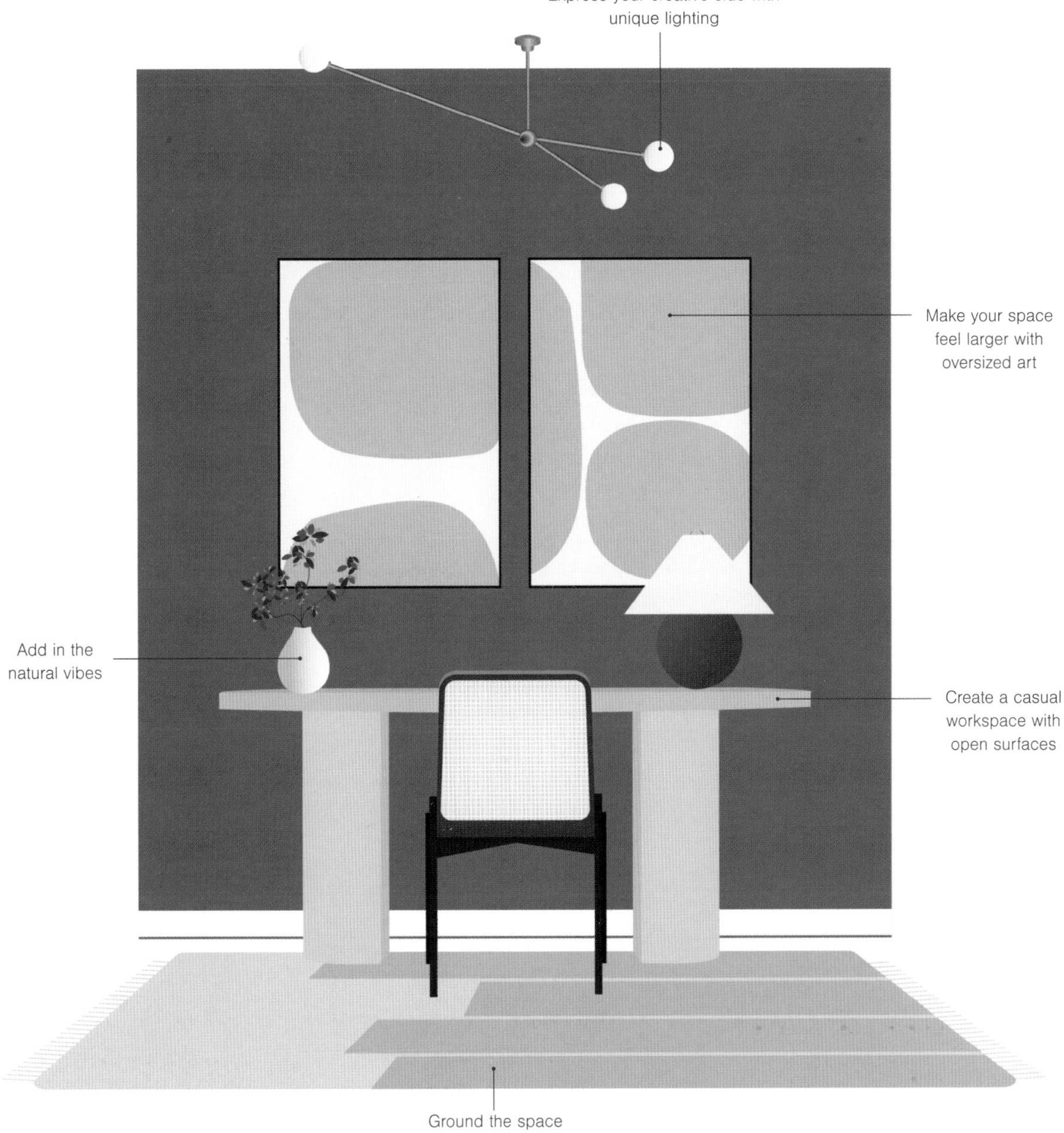
Express your creative side with unique lighting
Make your space feel larger with oversized art
Add in the natural vibes
Create a casual workspace with open surfaces
Ground the space

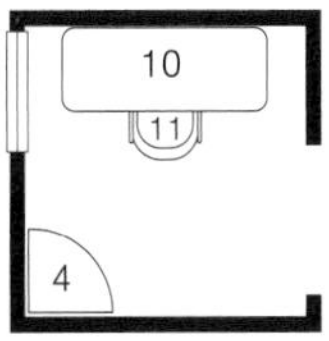
10
11
4

MINIMAL WORKS

7' W x 7' D

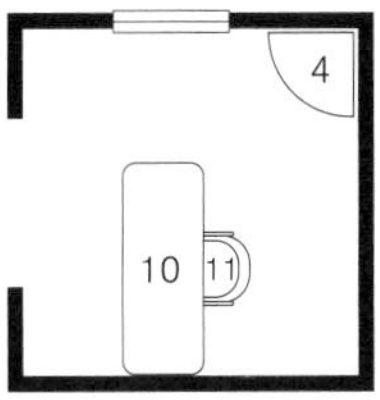
4
10
11

PROFESSIONAL FEELING

8' W x 8' D

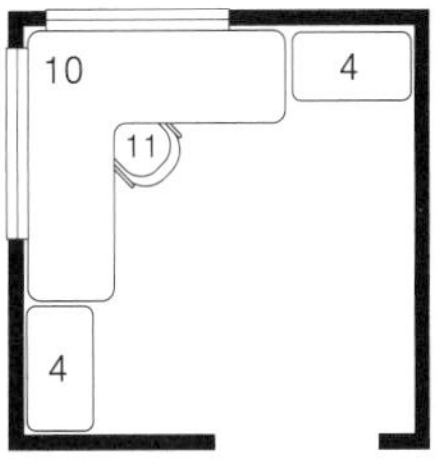
10
4
11
4

SPACE TO SPREAD OUT

10' W x 10' D

02. Choose your core components. Think about how much desk space you need vs. storage space. For the Minimal Works office, I chose an open desk and a corner storage unit.

03. Organize! The corner unit offers both open and closed storage space. The shelving works well for books and other office supplies that you don't mind keeping out in the open. The cabinet below hides away extra printer paper and other items you may want to keep out of sight.

04. Light it up. In this enclosed space, I layered the lighting. I used a semi-flush mount light to cast ambient light over the room. The low height of the desk lamp provides task lighting. Notice how the round shape of the base provides a counterpoint to the right angles of the desk and chair. Wall sconces flanking the artwork shed warm light onto the work area from behind.

05. Watch your step. I placed a rectangular rug beneath the desk. Make sure you choose a low-pile option so you can easily slide your chair in and out from your desk.

06. Accessorize. For inspiration throughout the day, layer in artwork, objects of meaning, and elements of nature. For me, natural light and plants are a must! I placed a vase with leafy branches on the desk and a little potted plant on top of the corner unit. Above the desk, I hung two large framed graphic pieces of artwork, and on the wall with the cabinet, I arranged three different-sized pieces for visual interest.

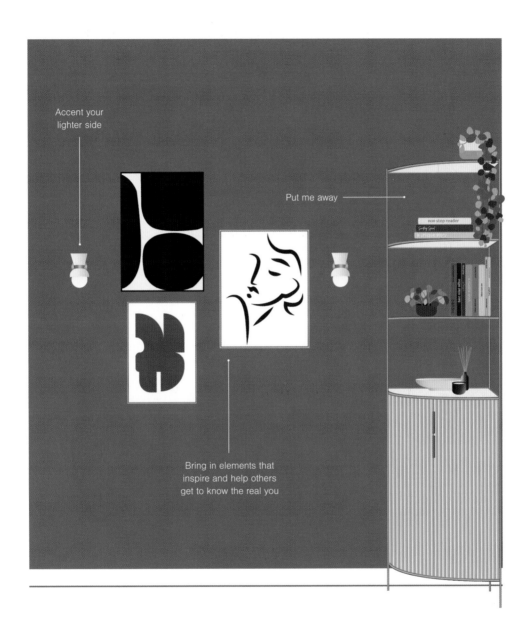

Accent your
lighter side

Put me away

Bring in elements that
inspire and help others
get to know the real you

# Medium / Large Office

Believe it or not, sometimes I find it more difficult to create a highly functional office in a larger space. But no stress—I'll show you the best tricks to make the most of your office without completely stuffing each nook and cranny or leaving too much empty space. The first step is to decide where to position your desk. Large rooms allow for desks placed in the center of the room, which makes a bold statement—but keep in mind that it means a fair amount of cable and cord maintenance! This recipe offers three different configurations for three different room sizes.

## What You Need:

| Heads Down Focus | Set for the Boss | Space for Collaboration |
| 12' W x 10' D | 14' W x 12' D | 13' W x 13' D |
| --- | --- | --- |
| (1) Desk: 60–72" W | (1) Desk: 60–72" W | (1) Desk: 60–72" W |
| (1) Desk Chair | (1) Desk Chair | (1) Desk Chair |
| (1) Credenza: 60–72" W | (2) Tall Cabinets: 36" W | (2) Guest Chairs |
| (1) Lounge Chair | (1) Credenza: 72" W | (2) Tall Cabinets |
| (1) Side Table or Ottoman | (1) Area Rug: 6' x 9' | (1) Bar Cart: 30" W |
| (1) Area Rug: 4' Round | (1) Semi-Flush Mount | (2) Bookcases: 30–36" W |
| (1) Flush Mount | (2) Sconces | (1) Area Rug: 8' x 10' |
| (2) Sconces | (1) Desk Lamp | (1) Semi-Flush Mount |
| (1) Desk Lamp | (1) Floor Lamp | (2) Sconces |
| (1) Floor Lamp | (1) Cable Management Tray | (1) Desk Lamp |
| (1) Creative Wall Treatment | (1) Cable Management Cord | (2) Floor Lamps |
| (1) Cable Management Tray | (1) Cable Management Floor | (1) Cable Management Tray |
| (1) Cable Management Cord | | (1) Cable Management Cord |
| | | (1) Cable Management Floor |

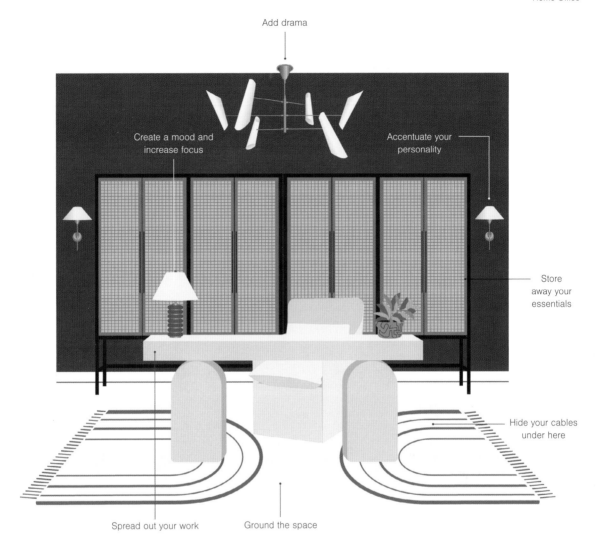

Add drama

Create a mood and
increase focus

Accentuate your
personality

Store
away your
essentials

Hide your cables
under here

Spread out your work

Ground the space

**HEADS DOWN FOCUS**

12' W x 10' D

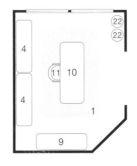

**SET FOR THE BOSS**

14' W x 12' D

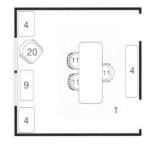

**SPACE FOR COLLABORATION**

13' W x 13' D

# Add-Ons:

| | | |
|---|---|---|
| (2) Floating Shelves | (2) Ottomans | (1) Layered Area Rug: 6' x 9' |
| (2) Bookcases: 30–36" W | Roman or Roller Shade | Puck or Strip Lights |
| Curtains | (2) Artworks: 24" W x 36" H | (2–4) Artworks: 16" W x 20" H |
| (2) Artworks: 24" W x 36" H | (1) Medium Plant | (1) Small Plant |
| (3–4) Baskets with Lids | (1) Writing Utensil Holder | (1) Trash Can |

01. Assess your space. Refer to your floor plan or sketch things out if that's helpful. Your sketch doesn't have to be perfect, and it will help you envision which elements will work for your particular space.

02. Choose your core components. For the Set for the Boss office, I positioned a desk with bold lines in the center of the room. On the wall to the side, I placed a low console with closed storage space. The upholstered chair brings warmth and softness to the room.

03. Organize! The tall cabinets behind the desk offer loads of space to keep all your office supplies easy to reach and out of sight. The height makes a dramatic backdrop for the desk. The low console also has closed storage space that can fit a small printer and scanner.

04. Light it up. Throughout the day, you'll need different light levels to work by, which can also help you stay in tune with your natural circadian rhythm. Bright light in the morning creates deep focus, but low levels at night might be just what you need for gaming! I spread the lighting throughout the room but concentrated it in the workspace with a semi-flush mount over the desk and a desk lamp for task lighting. The narrow rectangular base of the lamp echoes the shape of the desk legs. Two sconces flank the tall cabinets and shed warm light on the desk area from behind.

05. Watch your step. The large rectangular rug beneath the desk grounds the space and hides cables and cords. Make sure you choose a low-pile option so you can easily slide your chair in and out from your desk.

06. Accessorize. Don't fear color! Use it to let your personality shine through. You might start with a neutral base color and then add pops of color with accessories. For this office, I chose a deep hue for the walls. I hung two large, framed pieces of artwork above the console and arranged a shallow bowl, scented candle, and small vase on the top. I set a tall plant with lacy foliage on one side of the console and a shorter one with dense foliage on the other side for balance.

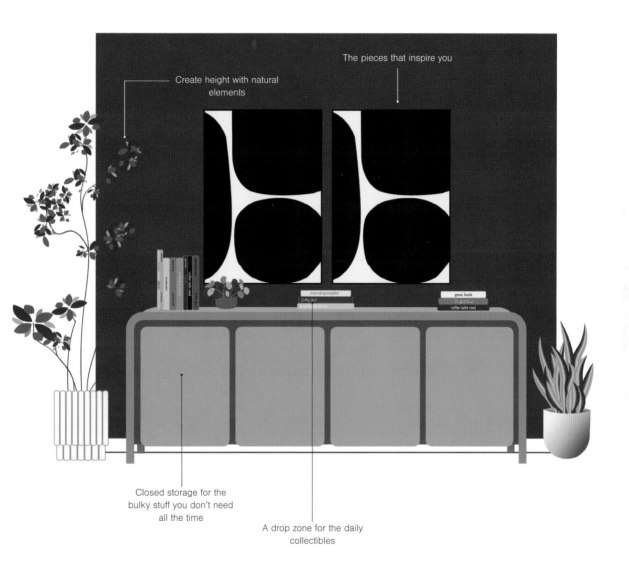

The pieces that inspire you

Create height with natural
elements

Closed storage for the
bulky stuff you don't need
all the time

A drop zone for the daily
collectibles

# The Shared Office

Sharing an office is no easy task! Whether you share the room on a daily basis or occasionally share it with a guest, it's important to carve out your own space. And organization is essential. Anything you can do to keep the space tidy will make it feel roomier. This recipe has two floor plans and ingredients for an office that doubles as a guest room, as well as one floor plan and ingredients for an office for two.

## What You Need:

| Made for Two<br>12' W x 10' D | A Guest Space<br>13' W x 10' D | Spare Bedroom<br>14' W x 10' D |
|---|---|---|
| (2) Desks: 48" W | (1) Desk: 60–72" W | (1) Desk: 60" W |
| (2) Desk Chairs | (1) Desk Chair | (1) Desk Chair |
| (1) Credenza: 72" W | (1) Mobile Storage Pedestal | (1) Mobile Storage Pedestal |
| (1) Lounge Chair | (1) Sleeper Sofa: 84" W | (1) Sleeper Sofa: 84" W |
| (1) Side Table or Ottoman | (2) Bookcases: 30" W | (1) Queen Bed |
| (1) Area Rug: 6' x 9' | (1) Laptop Side Table | (2) Nightstands: 24" W |
| (1) Flush Mount | (2) Ottomans | (1) Area Rug: 6' x 9' |
| (2) Sconces | (1) Area Rug: 6' x 9' | (1) Flush Mount |
| (2) Desk Lamp | (1) Flush Mount | (2) Sconces |
| (1) Floor Lamp | (2) Sconces | (1) Desk Lamp |
| (1) Creative Wall Treatment | (1) Desk Lamp | (1) Creative Wall Treatment |
| (2) Cable Management Tray | (1) Floor Lamp | (1) Cable Management Tray |
| (2) Cable Management Cord | (1) Creative Wall Treatment | (1) Cable Management Cord |
| | (1) Cable Management Tray | |
| | (1) Cable Management Cord | |

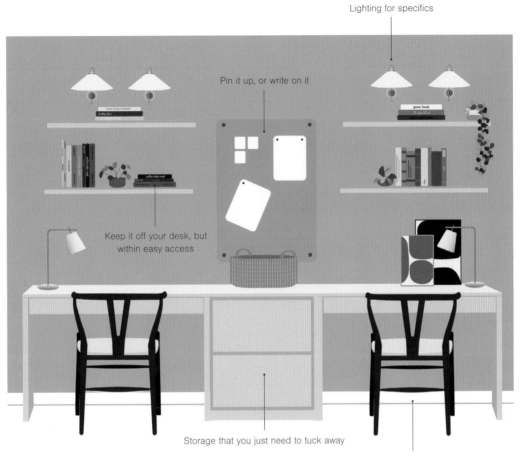

Lighting for specifics

Pin it up, or write on it

Keep it off your desk, but
within easy access

Storage that you just need to tuck away

A comfy chair that allows you to
spread out your work

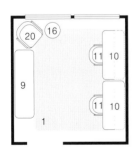

**MADE FOR TWO**

12' W x 10' D

**A GUEST SPACE**

13' W x 10' D

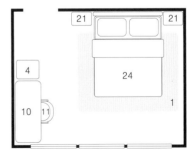

**SPARE BEDROOM**

14' W x 10' D

# Add-Ons:

| | | |
|---|---|---|
| (2–4) Floating Shelves | Puck or Strip Lights | Roman or Roller Shade |
| (2) Bookcases: 30–36" W | Curtains | (2) Artworks: 24" W x 36" H |
| (2) Artworks: 16" W x 20" H | (1) Medium Plant | (1) Small Plant |
| (3–4) Baskets with Lids | (1) Writing Utensil Holder | (1–2) Trash Can(s) |

01.  Assess your space. Refer to your floor plan or sketch things out if that's helpful. Your sketch doesn't have to be perfect, and it will help you envision which elements will work for your particular space.

02.  Choose your core components. For the Made for Two office, I chose a double-wide desk with room underneath for a filing cabinet. The cabinet creates a natural division of space for you and your office mate. I paired the desk with lightweight chairs that are easy to move around. A short open shelving unit sits next to a comfy chair and side table on the opposite wall.

03.  Organize. Floating shelves above the desk make for easy access to office supplies. The filing cabinet will keep your paperwork off the desktop and out of sight. You can toss extra supplies in the open baskets on the shelving unit.

04.  Light it up. Sconce lights above each side of the desk cast light onto the workspace. Ideally, you'll have separate switches for each side so each person can control their level of light. On the open shelves, I placed a small, squat table lamp. On the wall next to the chair, I mounted a double reading light. You can adjust the position depending on your needs. I recommend keeping window treatments minimal to allow natural light to flow in. Natural light makes for a healthy workspace and improves your day-to-day well-being.

05.  Watch your step. The large rectangular rug extends from beneath the desk all the way under the shelving unit opposite. It provides an anchor for the space. Make sure you choose a low-pile option so you can easily slide your chair in and out from your desk.

06.  Accessorize. When you share an office space with others, be respectful of your office mate and choose decor that's appealing to both of you. In this shared office, I placed a bulletin board in the center of the wall above the desk and I filled the opposite wall with framed artwork of different sizes for a bold, maximalist look.

Let your creative side shine

Add the element of surprise while saving space

Open storage with closed elements to tuck things away when you need to

Prepare to lounge around

# CHAPTER TWELVE

# Outdoors

Outdoor spaces can serve multiple purposes, providing a quiet space to relax and meditate on your own or a festive place to entertain friends and family. Whether you have a small balcony, a back patio, or a full-on front yard and backyard, these spaces are an extension of your home, and you can apply many of the same principles for a living room or dining room to your outdoor space. What a fun way to increase your square footage!

If you're on the hunt for the right outdoor dining table, head to the Dining Room section on page 126 and apply the sizing techniques to your outdoor space.

# The Balcony

Envision how you want to use your balcony. Will you use it to enjoy your morning coffee? Or perhaps you'll make it a sunny meditation station. You could also hang a hammock for a napping zone. Be sure to take into consideration the sides of your space. If you want to create privacy, consider using a few tall plants or bamboo shades. This recipe will show you how to make the most of your small space. I've included floor plans and ingredients for three different-sized spaces and diagrams for the two larger ones.

## What You Need:

| Setting for Two 4' W x 9' D | A Relaxing Space 6' W x 9' D | Lounge Around 7' W x 10' D |
|---|---|---|
| (1) Bistro Table: 24" Round | (2) Lounge Chairs | (1) Sofa: 72" W |
| (2) Dining Chairs or Stools | (1) Side Table | (2) Ottomans |
| | (1) Outdoor Area Rug: Round | (1) Outdoor Area Rug: 5' x 7' |

## Add-Ons:

| | | |
|---|---|---|
| String Lights | (1) Large Plant | Swap in a Hammock |
| (2) Small Plants | Outdoor Heater | Bamboo or Tall Plant Wall |
| Tray for Ottomans | | |

01.   Assess your space. Refer to your floor plan or sketch things out if that's helpful. Your sketch doesn't have to be perfect, and it will help you envision which elements will work for your particular space.

02.   Choose your core components.

   **AN INTIMATE EXPERIENCE:** This balcony had just enough room for two chairs and a small side table. I chose chairs with a low profile. The seats and backs are made of weather-resistant canvas.

   **LOUNGE AROUND:** I had a little more space to work with, so I chose an outdoor sofa and placed two ottomans in front to serve various purposes—you can use them for extra seating, a place to put your feet up, or a table for your drinks and snacks.

03.   Light it up. Most balconies have an outdoor electrical outlet. If yours doesn't, you can always use solar lanterns.

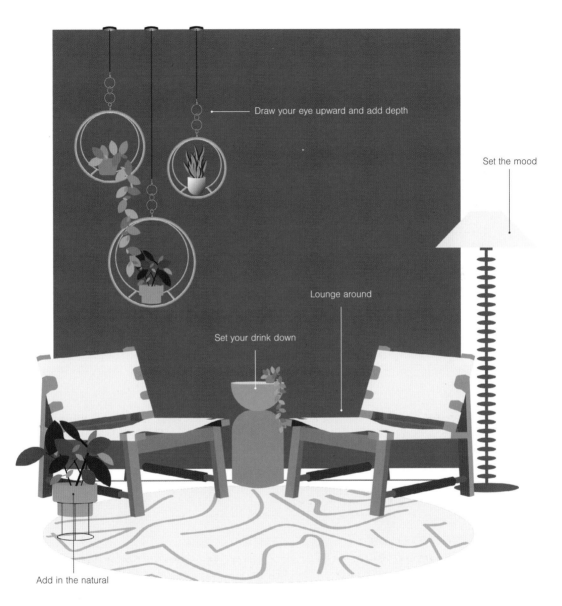

Draw your eye upward and add depth

Set the mood

Lounge around

Set your drink down

Add in the natural

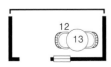

### SETTING FOR TWO

Seats 2 People
4' W x 9' D

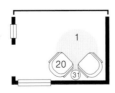

### A RELAXING SPACE

Seats 2 People
6' W x 9' D

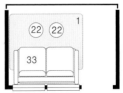

### LOUNGE AROUND

Seats 2–4 People
7' W x 10' D

**AN INTIMATE EXPERIENCE:** I placed a tall floor lamp beside one of the chairs for a cozy reading spot in the evening.

**LOUNGE AROUND:** A chandelier pulls the eye upward while casting soft light down onto the seating area. I placed two sconces on either side of the windows for warm accent lighting.

04.   Watch your step. Be sure to choose a rug that can stand up to the outdoors. And have fun with color!

**AN INTIMATE EXPERIENCE:** A round rug grounds the space and echoes the shape of the hanging planters.

**LOUNGE AROUND:** I chose a rectangular rug with a sinuous pattern to provide a counterpoint to the rectangular lines of the couch.

05.   Accessorize. In an outdoor space, plants are your star accessories.

**AN INTIMATE EXPERIENCE:** I placed a potted plant in an elevated stand next to one of the chairs and then positioned three hanging plants of different sizes above the seating area to draw the eye upward.

**LOUNGE AROUND:** The tall tree in a pot balances out the height of the windows. I chose a handsome ceramic pot with a pattern that complements the lines in the pattern of the rug.

Add soft accent lights to set the tone

Add height with plant life

No excuses, relaxation starts now

Put your feet up

Give yourself the cozy feeling

# The Small Oasis

With a bit of space to work with, you can create a welcoming space to entertain or dine alfresco. For this recipe, I included two different options based on the size of the space. Both feature bold overhead lighting for a strong style statement.

## What You Need:

| Intimate Outdoors<br>7' W x 7' D | Relax & Dine In<br>9' W x 9' D | A Lounge<br>10' W x 10' D |
| --- | --- | --- |
| (2) Lounge Chairs | (1) Dining Table: 48" | (1) Sofa: 84" |
| (1) Coffee Table: 30" | (4) Dining Chairs | (2) Accent Chairs |
| (1) Area Rug: 6' Round | (1) Area Rug: 8' Round | (1) Area Rug: 6' x 9' |
| (1) Side Table | | (1) Coffee Table: 48" x 24" |

## Add-Ons:

| | | |
| --- | --- | --- |
| (1–2) Ottoman(s) | (1) Grill | (1) Firepit |
| (1–2) Lantern(s) | String Lights | (1–2) Large Plant(s) |
| (2) Medium Plants | (2) Small Plants | (1) Outdoor Heater |
| (1) Outdoor Umbrella or Shade | | |

01.  Assess your space. Refer to your floor plan or sketch things out if that's helpful. Your sketch doesn't have to be perfect, and it will help you envision which elements will work for your particular space.

02.  Choose your core components.

03.  **INTIMATE OUTDOORS:** I chose an eclectic array of furniture. Nothing matches exactly, but the shapes and colors complement each other, which creates a harmonious feel. For seating, I paired a hanging swing chair with a cushy armchair. The low, round table provides a spot to put your feet up or lay out a delicious spread. A nesting table between the chairs makes for a handy spot to set your drink.

Create scale with
oversized lighting

A place to swing

Plant mom alert

A place to sit

Put your feet up or your wine down

Make it cozy

### INTIMATE OUTDOORS

Seats 2 People

7' W x 7' D

### RELAX & DINE IN

Seats 2–4 People

9' W x 9' D

### A LOUNGE

Seats 2–4 People

10' W x 10' D

04. **RELAX & DINE IN:** This space is all about dining alfresco. The round pedestal table is the center-piece and I've positioned cushy dining chairs around the table.

05. Light it up. Most balconies have an outdoor electrical outlet. If yours doesn't, you can use solar lanterns.

    **INTIMATE OUTDOORS:** The hanging dome light mirrors the shape of the coffee table and sheds a wide span of light over the entire space.

    **RELAX & DINE IN:** I chose a more formal chandelier to dress up this outdoor dining area.

06. Watch your step. For both of these spaces, I chose a round rug to ground the space. Be sure to choose a rug that can stand up to the outdoors. And have fun with color!

07. Accessorize. I like to use contrasting colors in outdoor spaces. For these two, I chose lighter-colored seating to contrast with the darker exterior walls. I also recommend extending style elements from interiors to your outdoor space. It could be a throw blanket in similar color to your living room, an ottoman in the same style as one you use indoors, or a piece of artwork that ties the indoors and outdoors together.

    **INTIMATE OUTDOORS:** Once again, plants are the superstar accessories. I went with a variety of sizes—a small potted succulent on the nesting tables, a leafy mid-height potted plant next to the swing chair, and a tall leafy plant in a handsome ceramic pot to balance out the height of the swing chair.

    **RELAX & DINE IN:** I chose not to use accessories in this outdoor area in order to keep the floor-space clear for the chairs, and the tabletop clear for enjoying meals.

Create a focal point with light

Add an accent wall

Ground the space

Get cozy and dine together

# The Medium Outdoors

With a fair amount of space to play with, you can feature a lot of seating. The trick is making the seating area feel cozy. Just because you have the space, doesn't mean you should spread out the key pieces. Don't be afraid to pull things inward to create a more intimate vibe! It's perfectly fine to center your seating area in the space and leave a wide perimeter around it. This recipe has ingredients and floor plans for three different-sized spaces. Feel free to take what works for you to create your own personalized space that serves your needs.

## What You Need:

| Lounge All Day<br>12' W x 12' D | Outdoor Socializer<br>12' W x 14' D | Expand Your Horizons<br>14' W x 16' D |
|---|---|---|
| (1) Sectional: 108" W x 108" L | (2) Sofas: 96" L | (1) Sectional: 132" W x 132" L |
| (1) Coffee Table: 36" Round | (2) Lounge Chairs | (2) Lounge Chairs |
| (2) Accent Chairs | (1) Coffee Table: 60" x 60" | (1) Coffee Table: 60" x 60" |
| (2–3) Side Tables | (2) Side Tables | (3) Side Tables |
| (1) Area Rug: 8' x 10' | (1) Area Rug: 10' x 12' | (2) Ottomans |
| | | (1) Area Rug: 10' x 12' |

## Add-Ons:

| | | |
|---|---|---|
| (1) Outdoor Fan/Chandelier | (1) Outdoor Umbrella | Structure(s) |
| (1) Grill | (1) Firepit | (1–2) Lantern(s) |
| String Lights | (2) Large Plants | (2) Medium Plants |
| (2) Small Plants | (1) Outdoor Heater | |

01.  Assess your space. Refer to your floor plan or sketch things out if that's helpful. Your sketch doesn't have to be perfect, and it will help you envision which elements will work for your particular space.

02.  Choose your core components. For Lounge All Day, I went with an L-shaped sofa and placed two low-slung chairs opposite.

Let the air flow

Set the mood

The natural elements

Feet up or drink down

Get comfortable

### LOUNGE ALL DAY

Seats 4–6 People

12' W x 12' D

### OUTDOOR SOCIALIZER

Seats 4–8 People

12' W x 14' D

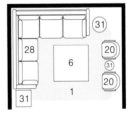

### EXPAND YOUR HORIZONS

Seats 4–8 People

14' W x 16' D

The circular coffee table is large enough to reach from all the seats. I put nesting tables on one end of the couch and a boldly shaped side table on the other end.

▶ **PRO TIP:** Face your furniture towards the prettiest view. That said, I don't recommend facing furniture toward the neighbors . . . awkward!

03. Light it up. The ceiling fan provides both overhead ambient lighting and air circulation for hot weather. A wall-mounted sconce directs light over one side of the sofa for a reading light.

04. Watch your step. The large square rug extends from under the couch to the chairs opposite. Be sure to choose a weather-resistant rug.

05. Accessorize. I kept the accessories simple with a tall potted plant on one side of the sofa and a small potted plant on the table on the other side of the sofa. The throw pillows add softness and comfort.

Insert s'mores here

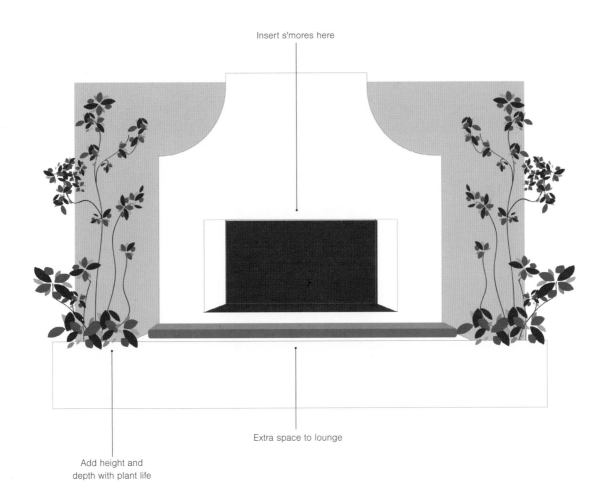

Add height and
depth with plant life

Extra space to lounge

# The Large Space

You can do so much with a large outdoor space. But it's easy to get overwhelmed with choices. The first step is to think carefully about how you'd like to use the space. If it's primarily for lounging you can create a relaxing feel with multiple seating or resting areas. If you like to entertain you could focus on a fully kitted-out dining area. Or, if you like to do both, you could combine a dining area with lounging area.

## What You Need:

| Dine in or Lounge Out<br>16' W x 18' D | Lay All Day<br>16' W x 18' D | A Dabble of Everything<br>16' W x 18' D |
|---|---|---|
| (1) Sectional: 108" x 108" | (2) Sofas: 108" | (2) Sectionals: 120" |
| (1) Coffee Table: 36" | (4) Lounge Chairs | (2) Lounge Chairs |
| (2) Side Tables | (1) Area Rug: 10' x 12' | (1) Area Rug: 10' x 12' |
| (2) Accent Chairs | (1) Coffee Table: 60" x 60" | (1) Coffee Table: 48" Round |
| (1) Area Rug: 8' x 10' | (4) Side Tables | (2) Side Tables |
| (1) Dining Table: 72" L | | (1) Dining Table |
| (1) Bench: 60" | | (4) Dining Chairs |
| (2) Dining Chairs | | (1) Area Rug: 8' Round |
| (2) Accent Dining Chairs | | |
| (1) Area Rug: 6' x 9' | | |

## Add-Ons:

| | | |
|---|---|---|
| (1) Outdoor Umbrella | (1) Outdoor Fan/Chandelier | (1) Outdoor Fan/Chandelier |
| (1) Storage Bench or Credenza | Structure(s) | (1) Grill |
| (1–2) Lantern(s) | String Lights | (4) Large Plants |
| (3) Medium Plants | (2) Small Plants | (1) Outdoor Heater |

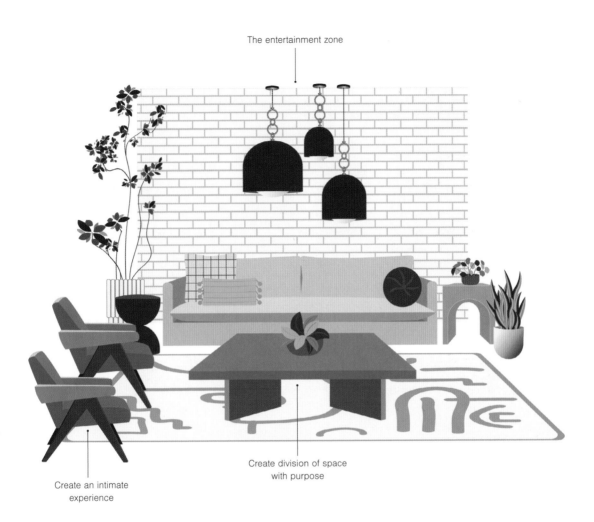

The entertainment zone

Create an intimate
experience

Create division of space
with purpose

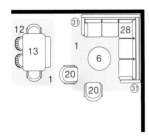

**DINE IN OR LOUNGE OUT**

Seats 6–12 People
16' W x 18' D

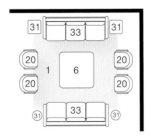

**LAY ALL DAY**

Seats 8–12 People
16' W x 18' D

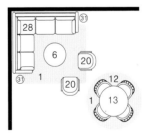

**A DABBLE OF EVERYTHING**

Seats 8–10 People
16' W x 18' D

01.   Assess your space. Refer to your floor plan or sketch things out if that's helpful. Your sketch doesn't have to be perfect, and it will help you envision which elements will work for your particular space.

02.   Choose your core components. Focus on the big pieces first and then choose the smaller pieces to fit the extra space.

03.   Light it up. If the sun beats down on your space, add an umbrella or two. The last thing you want is to have a beautiful outdoor area that doesn't get used!

04.   Watch your step. Rugs do a beautiful job of designating spaces. I placed a large square rug under the lounge area and then a smaller round rug under the table to differentiate the zones.

05.   Accessorize. I created height with a tall potted plant one on side of the sofa. On the other, I placed a smaller potted plant with dense foliage. On the coffee tabletop, I set a small potted plant that you can change out seasonally.

Perfect for visiting

Enjoy the sunrise with a
cup of coffee

Ground the space

## Footnotes

[1]Taylor, Lisa Hallett. "What Does 'FSC Certified' Mean?" The Spruce. The Spruce, May 12, 2022. https://www.thespruce.com/what-does-fsc-certified-stand-for-2736657.

[2]"What Does 'GREENGUARD Certified' Mean?" UL Solutions. Accessed November 2, 2022. https://www.ul.com/insights/what-does-greenguard-certified-mean.

[3]"What Is Cradle to Cradle Certified®?" Cradle to Cradle Products Innovation Institute. Accessed November 2, 2022. https://www.c2ccertified.org/get-certified/product-certification.

[4]"Durable Goods: Product-Specific Data." EPA. Environmental Protection Agency, December 21, 2021. https://www.epa.gov/facts-and-figures-about-materials-waste-and-recycling/durable-goods-product-specific-data.

[5]Rogers, Kara. "Biophilia Hypothesis." Encyclopædia Britannica. Encyclopædia Britannica, inc., June 25, 2019. https://www.britannica.com/science/biophilia-hypothesis.

[6]Alkahtany, Laila Amer. "Contribution to the Development of Interior Spaces in Hyperactivity and Distracted Attention: An Analytical Case Study." INTERNATIONAL JOURNAL OF DESIGN AND MANUFACTURING TECHNOLOGY 5, no. 2 (2014). https://doi.org/10.34218/ijdmt.5.2.2014.30320140502001.

## Acknowledgments

To the love of my life, Hammam Elkhoudary: Thank you for all your love and support during this wild creative journey. You are my biggest inspiration and I couldn't have done any of this without you. Thank you for challenging me, driving me, and being my guide when I needed it most. Thank you for your patience, kindness, and for holding it together in moments when I felt lost. None of this could have been imagined without you—my heart is full beyond what words can say. Each page of this book has your soul in it just as much as mine. I love you, always.

To Grandma Kay and Grandma B: Thank you for teaching me that strength and kindness go hand-in-hand. Thank you for teaching me that creating my own path was one to follow and not to ignore. I truly believe now that anything I put my mind to can be done, because of you. Thank you for driving me to become the person I am today, and for all the love you gave me in between. I love you more than words can describe.

To my sister, Anna Marx: Thank you for helping me write this book that was once just a pipe dream at my dining table. I can't thank you enough for spending countless hours listening to me rant about design and creating something with me that we can be proud of together. I love you so much, but just between us, I like you too!

## About the Author

Ariel Magidson is out to make sustainable design for everyone... no really, everyone! Thousands of social media followers use her design hacks and tips everyday for free. She created Ariel Arts to work within anyone's budget — from quick personalized advice to full-gut renovations, she's got you. With each project, she uses empathy to guide her designs to be approachable, sustainable, and affordable. Her commitment to sustainability pushes the boundaries of interior design to reduce waste and create beautiful spaces effortlessly. And the best part? It's all done virtually.

A Bay Area native, Ariel earned her BFA in Interior Architecture and Design from the Academy of Art University where she studied behavioral sciences and its unique correlation to design. To keep up the disruption pace, you can probably catch Ariel drinking far too much fair trade coffee around her favorite San Francisco neighborhoods.

**Blue Star Press.**

Cover Design by Arctic Fever Creative Studio

Interior Design by Megan Kesting

ISBN 9781950968916

Printed in Colombia

10 9 8 7 6 5 4 3 2